D0229335

WHISKY

3,000 BC onwards (all flavours)

© Tim Hampson 2015

All rights reserved. No part of this publication may be reproduced or stored in a retrieval system or transmitted, in any form or by any means, electronic, mechanical, photocopying, recording or otherwise, without prior permission in writing from Haynes Publishing.

Tim Hampson has asserted his moral rights to be identified as the author of this work.

First published in June 2015

A catalogue record for this book is available from the British Library

ISBN 978 0 85733 764 1

Library of Congress control no. 2014957383

Published by Haynes Publishing,
Sparkford, Yeovil,
Somerset BA22 7JJ, UK.
Tel: 01963 442030 Fax: 01963 440001
Int. tel: +44 1963 442030 Int. fax: +44 1963 440001
E-mail: sales@haynes.co.uk
Website: www.haynes.co.uk

Haynes North America Inc.,
861 Lawrence Drive, Newbury Park,
California 91320, USA.

Printed in the USA by Odcombe Press LP,
1299 Bridgestone Parkway, La Vergne, TN 37086.

Acknowledgement

With thanks to Cath Harries, whose original photography has brought this book to life.

FRONT COVER PHOTOGRAPH: By Cath Harries.

WHISKY

3,000 BC onwards (all flavours)

Enthusiasts' Manual

The practical guide to the history, appreciation and distilling of whisky

Tim Hampson

CONTENTS

(Cath Harries)

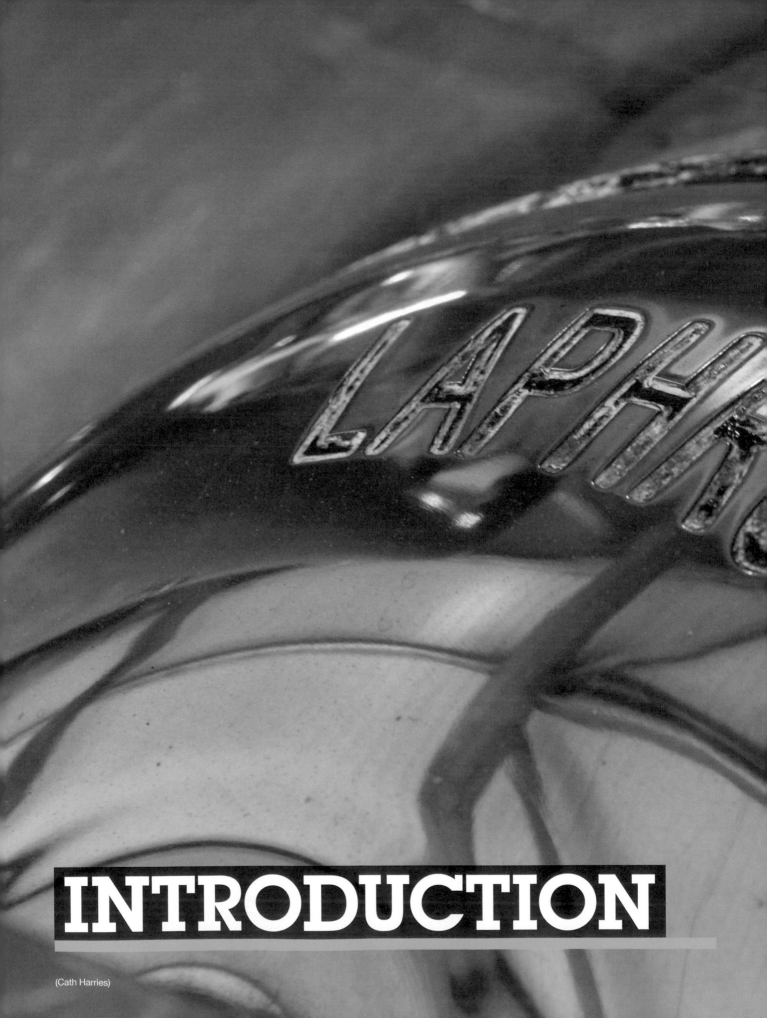

INTRODUCTION

(Cath Harries)

Time to take whisky seriously

If you go back a few years, vodka and gin were probably most people's spirits of choice, and Scotch and other whiskies were something kept in a cupboard for Dad to drink – and American variants like Jack Daniel's were for self-indulgent rock stars rather than ordinary folk. Now that has all changed.

Whisky of all kinds has become popular with older and more mature people as well as young, urban hipsters of both sexes. It takes barley, water and yeast to make whisky – but to make it great add in hospitality.

Whisky is not the easiest drink in the world to embrace. Its alcohol level is stronger than beer and wine and often the brand names are difficult to pronounce. But the drink itself, be it whisky or whiskey, has a range of flavours and aromas greater than any other distilled drink. At one end there are extreme smoky, peaty drinks with hints of tar and tobacco, while at the other end of the wide scale are soft, delicate, floral notes.

Just as none of us could ever pick up a saxophone for the first time and get a note out of it let alone play it, so it takes a little time and learning to embrace the world of whisky. But it is worth the effort. Whisky is more than just a drink: it is an adventure and its diversity should be explored slowly and indulged.

Whisky is made from grain and it is the story from the farm to the glass that is told in this book. It starts with a cereal, usually barley, which is transformed into a beer-like liquid, called wash, which is distilled. Distilling captures and concentrates the flavoursome, more volatile components in the wash.

But to this rich symphony, which some call moonshine or new-make spirit, we must add another ingredient – the wood that the whisky matures in, which brings profound influences in colour and flavour. The grains chosen, the distillation method and the casks chosen for ageing are the key factors that make every whisky different and alluring.

When HM Queen Elizabeth II launched the new class of aircraft carrier named after her from Rosyth Naval Dockyard in 2014, it was not champagne that she smashed on the ship's hull. Tradition was shunned and instead a bottle of Bowmore single-malt Scotch whisky wetted the side of the carrier. It was a symbolic confirmation that the time for whisky has come and a new age dawns.

It is time to take whisky seriously.

GETTING INTO THE SPIRIT

So what is whisky? The answer is not as easy as you might think. It is a spirit, which means that alcohol from a fermented liquid has been concentrated. But any fermented material can be used as a base material for a spirit, be it fruit, grain or another vegetable.

So what is in whisky? Whisky is made from a fermented cereal, such as malted barley. During the distillation process the base spirit for all drinks is pretty much the same – clear, neutral alcohol.

However, gin makers take the base sprit and then redistil it and add flavourings, such as juniper or coriander, or they might blend the base spirit with a concentrated distillate of botanicals. No ageing is needed: the liquid is diluted to bottle strength and off it goes. Vodka can be made from more or less anything, including potatoes and molasses; just filter it, add glycerine to give the liquid some body, and put it into a bottle. Akvavit and schnapps, north European favourites, can also be distilled from grain and then flavoured with spices such as aniseed or caraway.

So what makes whisky different? Unlike other spirits, whisky is matured in oak barrels, a process that turns the distilled spirit into a flavourful, characterful creation. Maturing in oak is the key to the character of whisky and makes it stand out from the crowd. Even the hardest oak is permeable and this allows the maturing whisky to breathe and oxidise, adding flavours to the spirit. The wood – whether new oak that has been charred or a cask that once contained bourbon or sherry – adds a cornucopia of flavour compounds and colours.

Whisky is a world drink and can be made in any country. A single-malt Scotch, however, has to be made and stored in oak casks in Scotland for at least three years, and it has to be produced in a certain type of still.

Most whisky in the world is made in a continuous-operation still, of which the Coffey (or 'patent') still is the most common; the Coffey is efficient and produces spirit of great purity. Scotch single-malt whisky, however, has to be double-distilled – or even triple-distilled – in a pot still, which is less efficient and more suited to small-scale production; this produces a base spirit with more character and complexity.

If you made the same drink in England using the same malt and a pot still and stored it for three years in oak barrels that once contained bourbon, you could never call it a Scotch. The name Scotch can only refer to whisky from Scotland. Perhaps there is an argument for calling an English whisky 'Englitch'?

The variety of whisky types can appear bewildering but there are four broad categories.

- **Single-malt whisky** This is made from a mash that contains only one grain, but the whisky in the bottle could have come from a blend of many different casks – unless it is described as a single-cask whisky.
- **Grain whisky** This tends to be made in a Coffey still with the base alcohol derived from cereals other than barley – such as maize, rye or corn.

■ **Blended-malt whisky** Just when you think you are getting used to the terminology, you will come across blended malts, which are made up of malts from different distilleries. If a whisky bottle's label states that the contents are malt or pure malt, it is almost certainly a blend.

■ **Blended whisky** A whisky blender brings together the output from many distillers so that a flavour consistent with a particular brand can be created. Most Scottish, Irish and Canadian whisky is blended, and blends are not uncommon in the US, where in some cases a neutral spirit can be added to the blend – a practice that is illegal in Scotland.

Most whisky is sold at 40% ABV (alcohol by volume), but one of the most recent developments is cask-strength whisky. This whisky might be blended, but it is only lightly diluted, if at all, making it stronger than most whiskies, typically 60–63% ABV. And from the growing popularity of the highly individual cask-strength whiskies comes the single-cask whisky, sometimes also called single-barrel whisky. These whiskies, which are bottled from a single cask, are also very individual, with wide variations in tastes and flavours from cask to cask, even when stored in identical conditions for the same length of time.

Every country where whisky is made seems to have its own local variations governing production and naming. Irish whiskey – note the different spelling – is traditionally pot-stilled

from a mixture of malted barley, unmalted barley and oats.

In the US, which shares the Irish spelling of whiskey, bourbon must be no more than 80% ABV by law, made from a mash of at least 51% maize, and stored for two years in new, charred oak barrels. Bourbon is derived from Bourbon County, Kentucky, but it can now be distilled in any US state; if a bourbon maker in Tennessee wants to call his product Tennessee whiskey, this can only be done if it has been filtered through charcoal, a method known as the Lincoln County Process. Corn whiskey – sold as 'moonshine' – must have at least 80% corn and is not normally aged, but when ageing is done it must be in uncharred new oak barrels or used barrels. Rye whiskey must have a minimum of 51% rye, while malt whiskey must be made from a mash containing at least 51% malted barley. Neutral spirits can be put into blends.

In Canada there is no restriction on the proportion of grains in a whisky, but it must be aged in barrels for three years and producers can add caramel if they choose.

Worldwide the production of whisky is strictly regulated but there are many variants on the 'breath of life' theme. However, whether a single-malt Scotch, Tennessee whiskey filtered through charcoal or a Japanese whisky, all will have been made of fermented grains and distilled and aged in wooden barrels. This variety is a joyful, vibrant part of the glorious, marvellous world of whisky.

(Cath Harries)

CHAPTER 1
THE WHISKY STORY

(Cath Harries)

A concentrated history of distillation

Did Jesus really turn water into wine? Or was this an early form of distillation? There is evidence that Babylonians in Mesopotamia in the second millennium BC were practising simple distilling, but others believe it began in China 1,000 years earlier. Certainly by 200 BC the Romans were boiling and bubbling ingredients to make concentrations of liquids.

But was this alcohol being distilled for drinking? It is more likely that the pioneer distillers were physicians and alchemists creating medicines, perfumes and balms. Many may have been making rose or lavender water, which were highly regarded for their medicinal and culinary qualities.

The equipment used was basic and probably not that effective or efficient. Steam probably rose from a boiling pot of petals and leaves and was collected in concentrated form in a lid of some nature.

There is definite evidence from Egypt by the first century AD of distillers being hard at work, but again they were not making a drink; they were making 'sulphur water' or 'divine water' as part of their experiments into turning base metals into gold. Another objective of early distillers was to create fire by means of these highly flammable concentrated liquids; fire was regarded as the highest and most important element. At some time these early distillers may have tried to distil liquids made from grapes or even cereals, but not to make a form of brandy or whisky – it would have been for flammability.

Dionysus, the son of the Greek god Zeus, was honoured with elaborate ceremonies at Delphi and other northern Greek cities from the fifth century BC. Wine was distilled and the flaming of the resultant liquid was part of the ritual used to honour the god of wine. Demeter, the Greek earth goddess who was responsible for fertile, well-ordered societies, was similarly honoured with rituals using grain.

This period gave us the alembic pot still (also known as the alchemical still), which is used for distilling chemicals and consists of two vessels connected by a tube. The liquid to be distilled is boiled in the first, slightly larger container and the vapour rises into the alembic hood, where it cools, condenses and runs down the spout into the other container. A modern-day spirit distiller would recognise this equipment as a pot still.

Moving on 1,000 years or so, to Bologna in northern Italy, word began to spread about a liquid with almost magical qualities described as *aqua vitae* – the water of life. It could cure colds, pains in the head, trembling, toothaches and even bad breath – and knowledge of *aqua vitae* spread quickly. At first Church authorities were not ready to accept medicines created by alchemy since they believed that illness was cured by God's will and not by physicians and apothecaries, but opposition gradually diminished and by the early 14th century many monasteries had their own stills for making *aqua vitae*. No doubt much experimentation occurred as the monks created medicines and healing liquids using herbs from their gardens – these were the precursors of modern liqueurs such as bénédictine and chartreuse. Monasteries were influential in the spread of knowledge about distillation, and at some time ale rather than wine would have been distilled in the search for new and better medicines.

By the late 14th century distillers in Italy were supplying distilled liquid to the public and many large households had

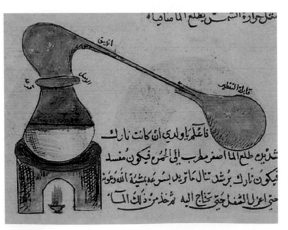

◀ The mystics used early stills to create divine water.
(Islamic Arts)

▶ Early stills produced *aqua vitae*, a liquid with magical qualities.
(Islamic Arts)

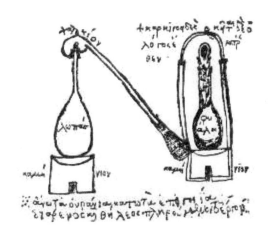

their own stills, causing the authorities to become concerned about the consumption of spirits as people without medical knowledge set up their own stills and sold spirit.

By the 16th century consumption was widespread and the national drinks of Europe had emerged: gin in England, jenever in the Netherlands and Belgium, schnapps in Germany, akvavit in Scandinavia, vodka in Russia and other parts of Eastern Europe, poitín (or poteen) in Ireland, rakia in the Balkans and ouzo in Greece.

The earliest documented record of distilling in Scotland is in 1494, when an entry in the Exchequer Rolls listed 'Eight bolls of malt to Friar John Cor wherewith to make *aqua vitae*'. The Gaelic translation of *aqua vitae* was *uisquebaugh*, which

▲ **Early commercial distilleries were usually remote, and places of some industry.** (Glenfarclas)

was known for its medicinal qualities, being prescribed for the preservation of health and the prolongation of life, and for the relief of colic, palsy, smallpox and a host of other ailments. It was given to babies, children and adults and over time it became better known by its name in English – whisky.

From cradle to grave – the fate of many Scots and whisky were forever entwined.

▼ **Since 1865 Glenfarclas has been owned and managed by one family, the Grants of Glenfarclas.** (Glenfarclas)

A little bit of Irish

Forget whatever people in Scotland may say. It is probably the Irish who gave us *uisge-beatha*, the water of life, the progenitor of the drink we now call whisky – and the Irish call whiskey.

▲ **Bushmills has been distilling on the same site since 1784.**
(Bushmills)

▼ **Spirits were valued for their medicinal qualities, and known as the breath of life – *uisge-beatha*.** (Cath Harries)

Ireland has the distinction of having the oldest surviving distilling licence – at the Old Bushmills Distillery. Bushmills was licensed in 1784, but distilling, legal or otherwise, was clearly taking place on the site for many years before.

It is believed that Irish monks brought alembic distilling for medical potions and perfumes back from their travels to the Mediterranean and Middle East around AD 600. Monasteries played a significant role in the development of most alcoholic drinks and it is understood that Irish abbeys were already distilling in 1170 when the armies of Henry II of England invaded Ireland, and it clearly became widespread as it is recorded that Irish alembics were already being taxed by the English in 1276.

POITÍN

So what was it they were making? Well, it was not stored for three years in used wooden barrels – that came much later. Possibly it was a drink similar to poitín (or poteen), an Irish drink that is one of the longest established spirits in the world, with a rich and turbulent history. Its production started in monasteries and then the skills and methods were

▶ **Alembic stills are often found in modern-day distilleries.**

(Cath Harries)

transferred into the wider community.

In 1661 the English Crown outlawed poitín because of the difficulty of taxing it and as part of a wider effort to repress Irish culture. This ban lasted for more than 300 years but the illegal status of the drink did not hinder its production in some parts of Ireland, for a widespread underground industry developed. Recipes were handed down through the generations, and the drink was secretly distilled and shared throughout that period. Over time it has become a symbol of Irish pride and independence.

The word poitín is Gaelic for 'little pots' – the small copper stills in which it is made. It is a raw spirit, or 'moonshine', that has traditionally been made from grain, sometimes barley, and later from potatoes, which were introduced into Europe in the 16th century. Poitín, which should have a pleasing herbal aroma, was most commonly produced in remote rural areas of Ireland. There were many techniques used in order to produce it without getting caught by the authorities. The fires required to heat up the wash were only burned on windy days to avoid attracting attention from lingering smoke, and the washes were often operated on the edge of land boundaries so that it was possible to deny ownership if they were discovered.

In 1989 it became legal for poitín to be exported from Ireland, followed by a change of legal status within Ireland in 1997. In 2008 the European Parliament and the EU Council gave Irish poitín 'geographical indication' status, which means that it must be produced in Ireland to be given the title Irish Poitín.

WHISKEY

The first confirmed written record of Irish whiskey comes from 1405. In the Annals of Clonmacnoise, a 17th-century English translation of a lost chronicle of Irish history up to 1408, the death of a chieftain is attributed to 'taking a surfeit of aqua vitae' at Christmas. It is recorded that Queen Elizabeth had stocks of Irish whiskey delivered to her court in 1541.

The modern Irish whiskey industry took shape in the late 18th and early 19th centuries. By 1886 there were 28 legal whiskey distilleries operating in Ireland, although there were probably hundreds more illegal ones. The whiskey was being sent to all parts of the world, particularly the US, Canada and Australia.

From about 1850 to 1915 Irish whiskey was king of the world, with the amount of whisky produced in Scotland miniscule in comparison to Ireland's output. However, the partition that came with the founding of the Irish Free State in 1922 and Prohibition in the US (1920–33) did for the Irish distilling industry and it all but died, on both sides of the border. Ireland's first golden age of whiskey was over.

The past 20 years, however, have seen a resurgence for Irish whiskey. Today there are about 20 distilleries in various stages of production, sales, planning and development. The biggest is Pernod Ricard's Jameson, followed by William Grant's Tullamore D.E.W., Jose Cuervo's Bushmills and Beam Suntory's Cooley distilleries. Sales are growing at 10% a year and booming in the US, Australia and Russia in particular, and annual output today is nearly 200 million bottles a year. A new golden age of Irish whiskey is here.

How the world got the whisky bug

Who would have thought that a yellow insect, closely related to the aphid, would kick-start whisky's rise to worldwide popularity after being unintentionally imported from North America to Europe in the middle of the 19th century?

Known as *Phylloxera*, this tiny, voracious bug feeds on the roots of vines, causing fungal infection, root deformation and eventually death. Also known as the 'dry-leaf devastator', *Phylloxera* is thought to have arrived in England during the 1850s on vines imported by plant hunters, but others say that a Frenchman, a Monsieur Borty, imported American vine cuttings and planted them in his Rhône vineyards in 1862.

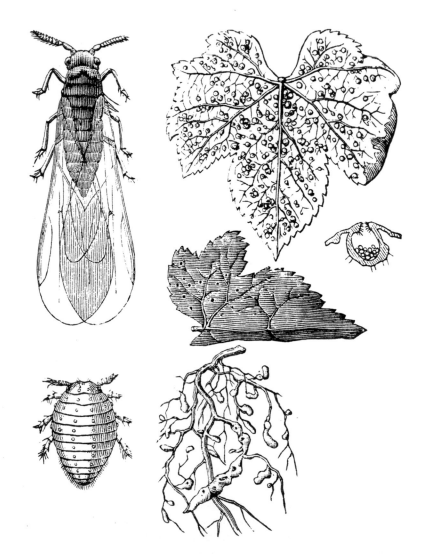

Whatever the truth, *Phylloxera* bugs went on to gorge their way through Europe's vineyards, causing so much devastation in France that the glory years of brandy came to an end. From Latin America to Tsarist Russia, French brandy was the drink of choice for the elite, and at the time millions of barrels of brandy were being imported into the UK annually, but within a few years the production of French brandy had all but ceased, with the vine-growing area of Grande Champagne, the home of cognac, wiped out by this plague.

But brandy's loss became whisky's gain. The Scots were quick to take advantage and by the time the French industry recovered Scotch whisky had replaced brandy as the spirit of choice. There are even records of port being fortified with whisky rather than brandy.

During the 1870s spirit merchants in the UK started blending whisky, by mixing spirit from the traditional pot still with grain whisky made in the new Coffey still. As pot-still whisky tended to be too strongly flavoured for everyday drinking by the elite, the addition of grain whisky, which has less pronounced characteristics, produced more mildly flavoured whiskies. The blenders probably had no qualms as to where the whisky came from or what piece of equipment it was distilled in, so spirit from Ireland and England was often added to the mix – although Scotch malts often underpinned these whiskies and provided the main characteristics of each blend.

The time for blended whisky – a drink of both sophistication and consistency – had come, with whisky and soda replacing brandy as the drink of choice for gentlemen. The Scottish whisky industry started to flourish, especially the blended sector, and by the end of the 19th century there were more than 160 working distilleries in the country.

◀ **A bug infestation of Europe's grape stock helped propel whisky to become a worldwide product.** (iStock)

History of the column still

Some purists will tell you that the spirit base of whisky can only be made in pot stills, but the reality is that most spirit is made in column stills. Usually faster and more economical, column stills are typically used for grain whiskies and produce a lighter, stronger spirit, as opposed to the heavier, fruitier bases usually associated with pot stills.

The alcohol to be distilled is made from a mix of malted and unmalted barley mashed with other cereals such as maize. As there is little or no malted barley, there are no malty or even peaty notes and other fruity flavours found with some spirit distilled in a pot still. However, since the malting, heating and maintenance costs of column stills are a fraction of those of pot stills, their use has had much merit to spirit producers.

In 1822 Irishman Sir Anthony Perrier wanted to find a distilling method that was faster than the pot or alembic still. Exports to America were growing and he was eager to develop a faster distilling process so that demand could be met. He patented a still that allowed the fermented mash to flow gradually and continuously over heat during distillation through a labyrinth of partitions; this procedure meant that small amounts of fermented wash received the greatest amount of heat, thereby increasing the amount of drinkable alcohol that was collected.

This invention inspired Robert Stein, owner of the Kilbagie distillery in Clackmannanshire, Scotland, to create a still that fed the wash through a column of partitions rather than the single chamber found in a pot still. Stein's single-column still, patented in 1826, never became a financial success, but Aeneas Coffey, who saw a demonstration of Stein's still, produced a column still of his own design and it became widely used. Coffey had worked as an excise man and during his long career tracking down illegal stills and visiting legal ones he had had plenty of time to observe various designs and their operation.

Coffey's design, which was patented in 1830, features two interconnected columns, named the analyser and the rectifier; in a large commercial distillery these columns can be about 20m high. Each column has two inlets, one for the alcohol containing wash at the top and the other for pressurised steam at the bottom.

The principle of distillation is relatively simple. When a liquid

▲ **Column stills revolutionised the making of spirits.** (Cath Harries)

containing alcohol is heated, the alcohol turns to vapour – and can be collected – when the temperature of the liquid reaches 78.4°C (at sea level), but the water in the liquid does not boil until the temperature reaches 100°C. Once collected and cooled, the vaporised alcohol returns to liquid form.

As the fermented liquid trickles down the first column of Coffey's still, it meets the rising steam, which strips out the alcohol. The now-vaporised alcohol travels to the top of the column and across into the other column to undergo a similar process. At the end of the procedure a highly purified alcohol of 85–95% ABV is obtained; the alcohol from a pot still is typically 68–73% ABV.

As well as producing alcohol of higher strength and purer taste, the column still has other advantages over the pot still. Unlike a pot still, it can be used continuously, without having to be emptied, cleaned and refilled after every use. It produces much greater quantities of alcohol more quickly than a pot still and it is cheaper and more efficient to operate.

At first rectifiers and gin distillers were the main users of column stills, but during the mid-1840s Scottish distillers started building Coffey stills in significant numbers. The more softly flavoured, cheaper whiskies produced from Coffey stills were much sought-after for blending with the fuller-flavoured, more expensive products of pot stills.

The whisky chaser

Alfred Barnard, who wrote about the wine and spirit industry for *Harper's Weekly Gazette*, decided in 1885 that he would visit every whisky distillery in the United Kingdom and describe his findings – the result was one of the most important books about whisky ever published.

Alfred Barnard was born in 1837, the year Queen Victoria ascended to the throne, in the tiny village of Thaxted, Essex, but, shunning rural life, he moved to London, where he pursued various careers, working as a draper and a wine merchant. At some time during the 1880s he changed career once more and started work at *Harper's Weekly Gazette*, the trade journal of the wine and spirit industry. The world of whisky would never be the same again.

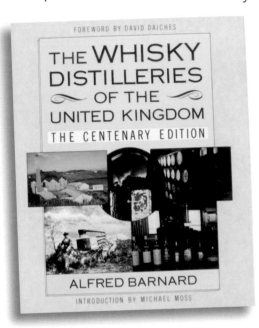

▲◥ **Alfred Barnard visited 162 distilleries to create his seminal book, originally published in 1887.**

The Victorians loved lists – whether of butterflies or breeds of birds – and Barnard's passion became distilleries. Early in 1885, while on a visit to the Scottish Highlands, he was struck by the fact that most of the world was probably ignorant about the places from where whisky came.

'At public sales and on the market generally,' read an editorial in *Harper's*, 'the make of Glen this and Ben that are freely referred to and dealt in, but how few know anything of the locality of the manufacturer connected therewith.'

Thus the idea was formed that he would visit every whisky distillery in the United Kingdom and describe its history, locality and method of working. Over a period of months his spirit of adventure and curiosity saw him complete a remarkable journey. By rail, boat, horse, coach and foot he visited 129 distilleries in Scotland, 29 in Ireland and four in England.

As a result of his work, in March 1887 *Harper's* published one of the most remarkable books about whisky – *The Whisky Distilleries of the United Kingdom*. In its 500 pages the book details many facts about each distillery, from the number of

▶ **Barnard chronicled the equipment and size of each distillery he visited.**

No. 24.

Glengyle Distillery, Campbeltown.

PROPRIETORS, WM. MITCHELL & CO.

MANAGING PARTNER, WM. MITCHELL.

AFTER breakfast the next morning we left the inn and got on the Distillery track again, this time bound for Glengyle. As we were proceeding leisurely up Longrow the occupant of a passing carriage hailed us, and on nearer acquaintance proved to be our old friend, Mr. John Ross. At his courteous invitation we joined him in a visit to the Provost and other Distillers, who like him were interested in the compilation of the book on which we were engaged, and assisted us materially in the object of our visit. After making an appointment to visit both his Distilleries in a few days, we left Mr. Ross to pursue his drive homewards, and continued our journey to Glengyle. On our arrival we found much to our chagrin that Mr. Mitchell was away from home, hence our visit was brief and our information concerning this Distillery necessarily somewhat scant. However the Brewer kindly proffered his services which we gladly accepted, and at once commenced our inspection of the place.

This Distillery is situate in Glebe Street, about one mile from the wharf, in the suburbs of Campbeltown. In front of the works there is a fine view of cultured gardens, cultivated fields, and hill slopes whose tops are covered with heather. The works were built in the year 1873 by the present proprietors. It is a neat and compact place, covering upwards of two acres of ground, and all the buildings are spacious and clean. There is a fine Barley Loft, two Malt Barns with Steeps; a Kiln, with wire cloth flooring, in which peat only is used for drying; a good Mill-house and Stores, a Mash Tun, 12 feet by 5, with patent revolving machinery, a 10-horse power Steam Engine, a Boiler 30 feet long and 9 feet in diameter; two Pot Stills, one containing 3,100 gallons, and the other 1,860 gallons; three Receivers holding respectively 2,500, 1,200, and 1,128 gallons, and three Warehouses holding 2,000 casks. There is a Morton's Refrigerator and a Force Pump. The Wash Charger holds 4,700 gallons, and there are six Wash Backs, each containing 6,600 gallons. A Spirit Store capable of holding 30 pun., and Vat containing 2,120 gallons; and the water used comes from the Crosshill Loch. Fourteen men are employed on the premises. The annual output is 90,000 gallons.

The Chief Excise Officer is Mr. James Douglas.

Gi'e him strong drink until he wink
That's sinking in despair ;
And liquor guid to fire his bluid,
That's prest wi' grief and care ;
There let him bouse, and deep carouse
Wi' bumpers flowing o'er,
Till he forgets his loves or debts,
And minds his griefs no more.

THE WHISKY
PAR EXCELLENCE.

Pattisons' distillers were quick to recognise the power of newspaper advertising.

employees to the quantity of production. Local photographers took pictures during Barnard's visits to provide reference for the artists who produced the etchings in the book.

'The object of this Work,' wrote Barnard in the preface to the book, 'is to give a familiar description and history of all the Whisky Distilleries of Great Britain, the product of which brings the largest revenue to the Imperial Exchequer of any industry in the Kingdom.'

Among the 129 Scottish distilleries, Barnard found that 120 used pot stills for making malt whisky and nine produced large quantities of grain spirit using the newly developed continuous-production Coffey stills. It was the marriage of whisky from different pot stills with the output from the Coffey stills that fuelled the great whisky boom of the late 19th century. With all its art and craft, blending made whisky – and in particular Scotch whisky – known all around the world.

Very few copies of the original book survive and the value of one is several thousand times the original price of one guinea (£1.05). A facsimile of the book, however, was published in 1987 to celebrate the centenary of Barnard's remarkable journey and there have been several reprints since then.

Following his whisky success, Barnard's sense of adventure saw him undertake a similar beer tour in which he visited over 110 breweries in the period 1889–91. This resulted in the book *Noted Breweries of Great Britain and Ireland*, published in four volumes over a period of three years.

Sadly many of the distilleries Barnard described have long since gone and even the buildings have disappeared. However, his remarkable work captured the whisky distilling industry at a time of growth and expansion as it became transformed from a farmhouse pastime to a large-scale commercial activity.

The late 19th century was boom time for whisky producers. Millions of gallons were produced and sold and millions more lay stored in barrels in warehouses. Sadly by the end of the century the whisky bubble had burst.

In 1898 one of the largest producers, Pattisons, went bust. The company had embarked on a worldwide advertising campaign that is said to have included a campaign in India in which 500 parakeets were trained to say 'Buy Pattisons' whisky'. On borrowed money, the company built new distilleries and bought existing ones, but it over-extended itself and crashed dramatically, dragging down with it scores of suppliers and other companies. The founders of the company, Walter and Robert Pattison, were later charged with fraud and embezzlement, but by then the damage was done and the glorious, burgeoning world described by Barnard went into a decline from which it took many decades to recover.

Prohibition in the USA

Prohibition – when legislators tried to stop Americans drinking – was a notorious time in the history of the United States. At midnight on 16 January 1920 the country went 'dry' and distilleries, breweries and drinking saloons were forced to close their doors – for 13 years.

The banning of alcohol was a long time coming. Ever since the first settlers came from Europe, there was always tension between those who liked alcohol and those who abhorred it as the demon drink. In the 19th century alcohol was highly taxed, driving many producers of spirits underground to make their moonshine illegally. Sadly, bootleg alcohol was often poorly made and sometimes contained creosote, lead toxins or even embalming fluid. However, it is said that one bootlegger, Bill McCoy, became well known for selling good-quality imported goods, giving us the expression 'the real McCoy'.

▼ **Police officers with distilling equipment and guns confiscated during a Prohibition raid in Chicago in 1929.** (Getty Images)

Temperance campaigners believed that banning alcohol would reduce crime, make people healthier and save taxpayers money as fewer prisons and poorhouses would be needed. Campaigning groups included the Anti-Saloon League and the Women's Christian Temperance Union, who argued that Prohibition would stop wife-beating, improve output from factories, and help make new immigrants more American.

The period of Prohibition, 1920–33, is often referred to as the 'Great Experiment', when legislators attempted to rid America of all alcoholic drinks by means of the Eighteenth Amendment to the Constitution. President Herbert Hoover enacted the legislation, stating 'our country has deliberately

▶ Patrons of a New York speakeasy in 1933 – the year Prohibition was abandoned. (Getty Images)

undertaken a great social and economic experiment, noble in motive and far-reaching in purpose.' Prohibition was widely thought to be a fine idea and even before the Eighteenth Amendment became law many states had already banned alcohol. America's entry into the First World War saw a patriotic outbreak of temperance: many breweries were accused of being run by Germans and in 1917 President Woodrow Wilson brought in partial Prohibition to conserve grain for the war effort; Prohibition campaigners said grain should be used for bread for fighting men and not for making liquor.

Prohibition did not work. Distilleries were either forced to close or driven underground, fuelling organised criminal gangs such as the one led by the notorious Al Capone in Chicago. Enforcing the law proved almost impossible, with smuggling and bootlegging becoming widespread. Rum-runners smuggled supplies of alcohol across state lines, and moonshine and 'bathtub gin' were commonplace. Bootleggers routinely bribed politicians and many police officers were on the payrolls of organised gangs.

According to one source, by 1927 there were an estimated 30,000 illegal speakeasies in America – twice the number of legal bars before Prohibition. But anyone wanting a tot of whisky could also go to a doctor and ask for a prescription for medicinal purposes!

Because the temperance movement taught that alcohol was a poison, it insisted that all positive mentions of alcohol should be eliminated from school books. A scholar was hired to rewrite the Bible – Jesus, it seemed, drank grape juice, not wine!

In one court case against an alleged bootlegger in Los Angeles, the jury drank the evidence – the tipsy jurors told the judge that they had to find out if it contained alcohol.

In the end Prohibition failed to deliver its promised benefits. The Great Experiment was unenforceable and within five years of its introduction six states, including New York, had passed legislation to prevent the police investigating breaches of the law. The American people were not going to let their freedom to drink be denied and the derided legislation was repealed on 5 December 1933.

'What America needs now is a drink,' declared President Franklin D. Roosevelt.

▶ Prohibition-era gangster Al Capone winks at the camera before facing a prison sentence of 11 years for income tax evasion. (Getty Images)

Blending in

In the mid-19th century Andrew Usher became the first commercially recognised whisky blender. His perfection of the art and craft of whisky blending helped to take the drink – at the time little known outside Scotland and Ireland – to worldwide popularity.

The passing of the Excise Act in 1823 encouraged many distillers to become traders. Prior to that most of Scotland's whisky was being made and drunk illegally, and according to some reports as many as 14,000 illicit stills were being confiscated each year. This mass flouting of the law led the government to realise that the only way to control the industry was to legalise it. The 1823 Act made it legal to distil whisky provided that a licence had been paid for and a payment was made for every gallon sold.

The new law laid the foundations for today's Scotch industry and saw illicit stilling and smuggling almost completely die out over the following ten years; indeed, several of today's distilleries are sited on land where there were once illegal stills.

As a wine and spirit merchant, Andrew Usher's father was perfectly poised to take advantage of the whisky boom.

In 1831 Aeneas Coffey invented the Coffey still (see page 17), which enabled a continuous process of distillation to take place. This led to the production of grain whisky, a different, less intense spirit from the malt whisky produced in the distinctive copper pot stills. Once the use of Coffey stills gathered pace, much of the whisky sold was a mixture of cheaper-to-produce spirit from a Coffey still and more expensive spirit from a pot still.

Increasingly people went to a wine and spirit merchant or a grocery shop to buy their alcohol. Much of it would have been stored in wooden vats and, as new spirit arrived, it would not have been uncommon for it to be poured into a barrel to create a new mix. When a customer bought whisky, it would be poured into a bottle at the time of purchase.

However, in an era of increasing consumer sophistication, the customers of the day came to want whiskies that were consistent in taste, quality and character, and it is Andrew Usher who is credited with creating a blended malt and grain whisky for the first time, around the middle of the 19th century, to produce a whisky of lighter flavour, extending the appeal of the drink to a wider market.

Usher was born in 1826 into a family of Edinburgh wine and spirit merchants, and his father – also Andrew Usher – had

◀ **Usher's was the first recognised whisky brand.** (Cath Harries)

▼ **Drinkers started to demand that their tipples were consistent in taste and quality.** (Old Sydney Signs)

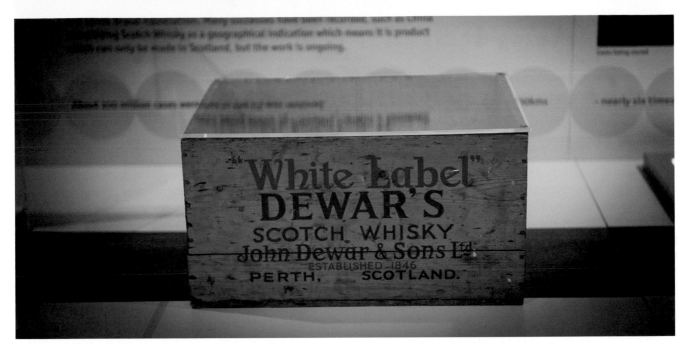

first experimented with the blending of whisky in the 1840s. At around the time of the younger Usher's pioneering efforts, changes in tax laws also made it easier to blend whisky in bulk and store it in a bonded warehouse.

It is thought that Usher's first commercial creation was sold in The Pear Tree, Edinburgh. He was the agent for Glenlivet, and he named his creation Old Vatted Glenlivet. By 1860 it was being advertised in London and by 1864 he was selling it to India.

Around this time others started to sell whisky in branded bottles. John Dewar is often credited with doing it first, but the Mackinlay family make that claim too. In fact there were many blenders – Johnnie Walker, George Ballantine, John Haig and Arthur Bell among them – who began putting their whiskies in branded bottles at about the same time.

Later, in 1885, Usher was one of the three founders – and chairman – of the North British Distillery along with John Crabbie of Crabbie's Green Ginger and William Sanderson of whisky distiller Vat 69. Their site on the western side of Edinburgh was ideal for blenders and sellers of own-brand whiskies who wanted to have access to their own supply of grain spirit for blending – and rather than buy it from others, they could make it themselves. Their spirit, unlike the alternatives, would be of consistently high quality at a price that they could control. Furthermore, the North British Distillery was perfectly poised to create blended whiskies for a new market in France, where the brandy industry was all but wiped out by the devastating *Phylloxera* (see page 16).

Andrew Usher became a very rich man and, like many wealthy people of his time, he became a philanthropist. He bequeathed £100,000 to the City of Edinburgh to build the Usher Hall, which was completed in 1900, two years after his death.

▲ **Sir John Dewar created the Dewar's whisky brand in 1846.**
(Scotch Whisky Association)

◀ **A famous old blend Black & White whisky was first blended in London.**
(Cath Harries)

▼ **Bell's famous blend is a mix of grain and malt whiskies.** (Cath Harries)

The native spirit of America

How did bourbon get its name and who invented it? The truth is that we do not know. There are as many competing claims for its origin as there are ways of drinking this corn-based whisky – which, as it is as American as apple pie, should probably be spelt 'whiskey'.

The origins of the drink, whose spiritual homeland is Kentucky, are not clear – and some of the stories seem more fanciful than others. But we really do not know how it got its name or who distilled it first or what it has to do with a French royal family, the Bourbons, most of whom lost their heads in the French Revolution – an ironic demise for a dynasty that had supported the American War of Independence.

So where does the French connection come from? What we now call Kentucky was originally the Kentucky District of Virginia. Because Americans were indebted to France for helping them defeat the English and win their independence, the grateful Virginian lawmakers gave parts of their territory French names. So it was that in 1785 came the creation of

▼ **Bourbon matures in oak barrels charred on the inside.**
(Cath Harries)

Bourbon County, which was an area much bigger than today's county of the same name.

The invention of the drink bourbon is often credited to a multi-talented Baptist minister called Elijah Craig. He must have been quite a man, as he is often cited in many Kentucky 'firsts', including the state's first paper mill and the establishment of the first school west of the Appalachians. Between sermonising, Craig set up a still in 1789 in Georgetown, Kentucky, and began producing whisky from a base of corn (maize). Others also credit him for hitting on the idea – either by serendipity or design – of using charred oak barrels in which to mature his spirit; charring of the oak gives bourbon its colour and taste. According to legend, Craig's still is said to have been one of the first in Kentucky and drinkers in nearby towns named his spirit Bourbon County Whiskey.

This story has much popularity, especially in parts of

Kentucky, but it has little credibility with many historians. A man called Elijah Craig certainly existed and he was a distiller and he clearly did many good things, but there is no evidence that his whisky was any different from any other – and his distillery was never in Bourbon County. Moreover, the charring of barrels was nothing new, for Europeans had been doing it for many years. For rather like the story of whisky, there was probably no single inventor of bourbon, the drink instead developing into the form we know today over a long period of time.

Immigrants to America from Europe certainly brought distillation to the New World. Early settlers put down roots in Central America and the Caribbean, and, unsurprisingly, started to make rum, which was a distillation of the widely available molasses. As time went by, more and more European immigrants started to populate North America and large populations were soon established around New York, Philadelphia and Boston. Barley, rye and wheat grew well in the east and distilleries quickly developed in the states of Maryland, Pennsylvania and Virginia; by the 1850s there were already more than 3,000 registered stills in Pennsylvania.

As settlers moved west, corn – a staple for native Americans – was found to be easier to grow than other grains and so it naturally came to be used by both the brewer and the distiller, who would frequently mix it with other cereals.

Distilling was certainly popular within the area of Kentucky through which the Ohio river flows to join the Mississippi on its way down to New Orleans. Barrels of whisky shipped down-river would often be marked 'Old Bourbon' to show their port of origin in Kentucky. Over time the mark 'Old Bourbon' became synonymous with whisky in the same way that the geographical names Cheddar, Parmesan and Champagne have passed to two cheeses and a fizzy wine.

Another interpretation disputes the idea that bourbon is a drink originally produced in an area known as Old Bourbon, in upstate Kentucky. According to the Filson Historical Society, which has a collection of bourbon labels from the 1850s, the story that the name bourbon comes from Bourbon County does not even start appearing in print until the 1870s.

Instead, it is said that the origins of the name are in New Orleans. Two traders known as the Tarascon brothers, who came from Cognac in France, began shipping whisky down the Ohio to sell to French immigrants as an alternative to brandy. One of the most famed areas in New Orleans, known for its music, bars and intemperate behaviour, was Bourbon Street. According to this version of the drink's history, revellers wanted more of the whisky that was sold on Bourbon Street.

And so a legend with many fathers was born.

This American fable of one of the world's greatest alcoholic drinks has two strands that weave through it like a 12-bar blues number – the distillate is made primarily from corn and it is aged in charred oak barrels.

The maturing of bourbon in barrels must have taken many years to develop. Resourceful farmers and entrepreneurs back in the 18th century were doing their best to survive in a harsh climate and an often-tough landscape, where barley and potatoes would not grow particularly well. But corn thrived and with it they could make a whisky – and at some time in the mid-19th century, possibly around 1840, some people started to call it bourbon.

However, it was not until more recent times that the name bourbon became codified in law and recognised as a product unique to America. In 1964 Congress recognised bourbon as a 'distinctive product of the United States' that could be made in any state. Even though there are nowadays makers of bourbon in California and Washington, 95% of all bourbon made still comes from Kentucky. It has to be made with a minimum of 51% corn, with the remainder being wheat, rye and/or malted barley, and the spirit must be matured in a new, charred oak barrel and sold at 40% ABV.

And, above all, it is meant to be sipped and savoured.

▶ **Buffalo Trace has been distilling for more than 200 years, and is the oldest continuously operating distillery in America.** (Sazerac)

For the love of peat

Many whiskies are characterised by intriguing phenolic flavours. Derived from drying malted barley in a kiln that has been heated with peat, these flavours are often described as medicinal.

Found in Scotland, Ireland, Canada, Finland and Russia, peat is an accumulation of partially decayed vegetation or organic matter that is unique to natural areas called peatlands or bogs. A peat bog grows by approximately 1mm per year, so a bog that is three metres thick could easily be 3,000 years old. When dug and dried, peat can be used as a natural fuel because it burns easily.

In both Ireland and Scotland peat was used for heating pot stills. It was readily available and relatively cheap, and able to generate the fierce heat necessary for distilling. However, this use of peat is not what leads to the smoky taste of the whisky; the flavours are created when the malt is dried in a kiln heated by burning peat.

The smoke from burning peat is a vital, vibrant contributor to the complex flavours of many whiskies, bringing sweetness, smokiness and abundant phenolic characters. Smoke from the fire drifts upwards through a wire mesh floor to dry out the barley and imparts a distinctive aroma that is sometimes known as 'peat reek'. These peaty aromas pass through the process into the distilled product and contribute to the character of the final spirit in a drinker's glass. The depth of the flavours is controlled by the length of time that the barley is exposed to the smoke.

No two peat bogs are the same. Peat harvested close to the sea on Islay may be salty and rich in decomposed seaweed, whereas peat from elsewhere may be more woody in flavour.

▼ **Smouldering peat brings swirling, smoky flavours to whisky malt.** (Cath Harries)

▼ **Peat was originally a cheap form of fuel, but today it brings character to whisky.** (Cath Harries)

▲ **Thousands of years old, many traditional peat bogs are still cut by hand.** (Cath Harries)

▲ **On Islay, stacks of peat waiting to be taken to a distillery are a common site.** (Cath Harries)

The Laphroaig distillery on Islay has its own peat beds and the peat is still cut traditionally by hand. This peat is made up of heather, mosses and lichens, a combination that makes for a different quality and flavour. The lichens give the medicinal flavours that are a hallmark of Laphroaig.

Peat holds the key to the distinctive flavours of many whiskies. Distilleries without maltings will source their peated malt from commercial malting companies and decide the

degree of 'peatiness' required, ranging from none to heavily peated. The level of phenol in the malt is measured in parts per million (ppm) and can vary from around 0.5–3ppm at the lower end to more than 80ppm at the other extreme.

▼ **Islay whiskies are famed for being some of the most peaty in the world.** (Cath Harries)

CHAPTER 2
THE WORLD OF WHISKY

(Cath Harries)

All in the name: the family of whiskies

Whisky, whiskey, bourbon and rye. Straight wheat, corn and white dog. Blended, grain, small batch and pot. The world family of whisky has many members and can be confusing, but all are based on a distilled spirit made from cereal (though sometimes sugar is used as a substitute), water and yeast.

There is a world of difference between whiskies – it is a drink known the world over and often defined by local culture and legislation. This section describes the main members of the whisky family.

▼ **The world of whisky is large, wide and has many family members.** (Cath Harries)

SCOTCH WHISKY

Scotch whisky has to have been matured for at least three years in Scotland in an oak vessel not exceeding 700 litres. Nothing can be added to it other than water and caramel. And currently the Scotch Whisky Regulation states that no other type of whisky can be made in Scotland other than Scotch.

Single-malt

A single-malt Scotch whisky will have been distilled using a pot still at a single distillery from water, malted barley and yeast, without the addition of any other cereals. It is distilled in batches and examples include Talisker, Dalwhinnie and Lagavulin.

Single-grain

Single-grain Scotch whisky is made from other grains as well as barley. It is made in a continuous still and has a lighter, more subtle flavour that makes it ideal for blending. Single-grain whiskies are distilled in one distillery from water and malted barley with or without whole grains or other malted or unmalted cereals. There are very few single-grain Scotch whiskies available but one example is Cameron Brig.

Blended

Blended whisky is Scotland's best-selling spirit and currently accounts for 90% of the country's whisky production. A Scotch blend is made up of both malt and grain whisky. The grain whisky, distilled in a column still, is easy to produce. It is a little more neutral in taste, so the malt whisky is added to the blend for flavour and body. Blended whiskies are defined under the Scotch Whisky Regulations as 'a combination of one or more single-malt Scotch whiskies with one or more single-grain Scotch whiskies'. Some examples are J&B, Johnnie Walker Black Label and Bell's.

Blended malt

A blended malt is a blend of single-malt whiskies that have been distilled at more than one distillery. One such is Johnnie Walker Green Label, a mix of several single-malt Scotch whiskies including Talisker, Caol Ila, Linkwood and Cragganmore.

Vatted malt

Vatted malt whisky is a term no longer recognised by the Scotch Whisky Association but it can be found on old bottles and in literature. Vatted malt describes a blend of single-malt Scotches sourced from more than one distillery.

Blended grain

This is a blend of single-grain whiskies that have been distilled at more than one distillery.

▲ **There are many variations to Glenfiddich's single malt range.** (Cath Harries)

▼ **Johnnie Walker's Double Black is a famed blended whisky.** (iStock)

▲ Irish whiskey must be stored in a wooden cask for three years. (Cath Harries)

IRISH WHISKEY

Irish whiskey must be distilled and aged on the island of Ireland and stored for three years in wooden casks.

Single pot-still whiskey

Distilled from a mash of both malted and unmalted barley, single pot-still whiskey must be produced in pot stills from just one distillery.

Single-malt whiskey

Irish single-malt whiskey is aged in oak for at least three years, and must be distilled from a mash of nothing other than malted barley at a single distillery.

Grain whiskey

Irish grain whiskey is distilled from one or more of the following: corn, wheat, rye and barley. It may be produced in any kind of still, although it is typically distilled in a column still.

Blended whiskey

Blended whiskeys in Ireland can be made by blending malt whiskey and grain whiskey, or also by blending single pot-still Irish whiskey with either or both of those other two styles.

AMERICAN WHISKEY

Big flavours often dominate American whiskeys. Lots of burnt oak, spice and vanilla can all be found. The use of new oak barrels, exclusively for bourbon, contributes many of these flavours.

In addition to barley-based spirits, there are also spicy rye whiskeys and charcoal-filtered Tennessee whiskeys, as well as a new wave of smaller craft distillers producing 'white dog' spirit, small-batch bourbons and straight corn.

Bourbon whiskey

Is this the spirit of America? Bourbon must be at least 51% corn in the selection of grains for distillation, there must be no caramel colouring, and it must not be distilled to more than 80% ABV. A bourbon is often characterised by thick vanilla sweetness, orange and other citrus notes, and some spicy hints like Christmas cake. Bourbon can be made anywhere in the US but Kentucky is where it was perfected.

Bourbon must be matured in new, charred white oak barrels. Due to the warmer climes in which it is made, it also matures much more quickly than Scotch and there is no minimum specified duration for its ageing period, with spirits aged for as little as three months sold as bourbon. The exception, however, is straight bourbon, which must be aged for at least two years; any straight bourbon aged for less than four years must state the age of the spirit on the bottle.

Blended bourbon can have added colouring and flavouring, and incorporate other spirits such as unaged neutral grain spirits, but at least 51% of the product must be straight bourbon.

Single-barrel whiskey

This whiskey is the darling of the new wave of craft distillers. It is aged in a single barrel and then bottled unblended. As single-barrel whiskeys are often bottled at cask strength – straight from the barrel – they can be fearsome, rich, complex and totally beguiling.

Rye whiskey

American rye whiskey must be made from a mash comprising at least 51% rye plus wheat and corn. An easy-growing cereal, rye gives the spirit its dry spiciness. It is distilled to no more than 80% ABV and aged in charred, new oak barrels; the whiskey must be put into such barrels at no more than 62.5% ABV. Rye whiskey that has been so aged for at least two years may be further designated as 'straight'.

Rye is the base spirit for many classic American cocktails, including the Manhattan, Old-Fashioned and Sazerac.

Tennessee whiskey

Made only in Tennessee, this is a sour-mash whiskey that is filtered through sugar maple charcoal prior to ageing using a technique known as the Lincoln County Process. The sour-mash technique – used in the preparation of most, if not all, straight whiskey – involves seeding a new batch of mash with a portion of a previous mash, which often has a sour taste. However, this does not mean that the resultant whiskey tastes sour.

Straight wheat whiskey

Different from bourbon, this is distilled from a minimum of 51% wheat. One of its exemplars is Bernheim, which says that wheat whiskey is the first truly new variety of American straight whiskey introduced since Prohibition. Wheat whiskey can be characterised by a smooth gentleness and some honey flavours.

Small-batch whiskey

Sometimes called single-barrel whiskey, this is as hard to define as craft whiskey; a production batch is usually under 20 US barrels. Well-known small-batch whiskeys include Maker's Mark, Basil Hayden's, Four Roses and Elijah Craig. Each batch is intended to be an exemplar of whiskey production and, needless to say, usually has a high price tag to match.

Straight corn whiskey

Straight corn whiskey is distilled from a mash bill of at least 80% corn. These whiskeys are not usually aged in new, charred oak barrels, as bourbon has to be. Most straight corn is matured for two years, but some is given very little time for ageing, a matter of weeks rather than months. The relative cheapness of corn made it a favourite of moonshine makers using illicit stills.

▶ **America's first distillers used locally grown corn as an ingredient.** (Cedar Ridge)

▲ **Big, robust flavours usually dominate America's famed whiskey and rye.** (Cath Harries)

White dog spirit

'White dog' is the name for unaged whiskeys, which are often called moonshine. It is a favourite of many of the new wave of artisan distilleries. These whiskeys are usually full of cereal sweetness and perfume fragrances. It is whiskey before the wood takes over.

The world's leading spirit producers

The world of whisky is dominated today by brands owned by multinational companies that span the globe. Like it or not, your favourite tipple, whether it is a genuine bourbon, an Irish whiskey or a perfectly crafted single-malt Scotch, is likely to be owned by one of these large companies.

In this section the world's leading spirit producers are outlined. It may be a surprise to find some of the biggest producers in the world come from India and have names that may be unfamiliar to you.

ALLIED BLENDERS AND DISTILLERS (ABD)

According to industry estimates, the Indian liquor industry is currently producing around 300 million cases per annum and is growing at 2–3% annually. It is a massive market and one of its biggest players is Mumbai-based Allied Blenders and

Distillers, which was founded in 1986 but remains little known in the western world.

According to some analysts ABD's flagship brand, Officer's Choice, a blend of Indian malt spirit and Indian neutral spirit, is currently the largest-selling whisky in the world. A recent addition to the company's line-up is Officer's Choice Blue, created by blending Scotch malts with select Indian grain spirits.

In addition to whisky, ABD makes brandy, rum and vodka, and also exports its products to the Middle East, South-East Asia and Africa.

◀ **Brands like Chivas Regal star on a world stage.** (Pernod Ricard)

▶ **Japanese whisky can trace it roots back to the Scottish Highlands.** (Beam Suntory)

BEAM SUNTORY

Formed in 2014, Beam Suntory is the latest mega-sized world spirit company and was created when Suntory, a Japanese brewing and distilling group, raised the finance to fund a £10 billion purchase of US spirits company Beam Inc. It is the world's third largest group, behind Diageo and Pernod Ricard, and is the custodian of brands that have heritages measured in centuries.

In 1795 a Kentucky farmer and grain mill operator named Jacob Beam produced the first barrel of a whiskey that he named Jim Beam. Suntory was founded in 1899 when Shinjiro Torii started selling imported wines; he went on to expand his business, against the advice of just about everyone, by building Japan's first malt whisky distillery, which began production in 1924 and sold its first single-malt five years later.

▶ **Whisky is a key component of some of the world's most famed cocktails.** (Beam Suntory)

▼ **Across the world, whisky is seen as a drink with style and distinction.** (Beam Suntory)

▲ **Laphroaig's famed peaty malts are now owned by Beam Suntory.** (Cath Harries)

Beam Suntory's product glass is well and truly full as it owns bourbon, Japanese, Canadian, Scotch and Irish whiskies. At the top of the pile is Jim Beam, the best-selling bourbon in the world that is now overseen by seventh-generation Beam master distiller Fred Noe. The group has a range of small-batch and speciality bourbons including Maker's Mark, Red Stag by Jim Beam, Jacob's Ghost, Knob Creek and Basil Hayden's. Beam Suntory also owns other

▼ **Teacher's Highland spirit thrives under international ownership.** (Beam Suntory)

category-leading whiskies: in Japan they include Yamazaki (the pioneer of Japanese whiskies) and Hibiki; Scotch brands are Laphroaig (the number one Islay single-malt), Bowmore and Teacher's; and other brands include Canadian Club, DYC of Spain and the Irish Kilbeggan.

BROWN-FORMAN

Brown-Forman produces some of the planet's best-known brands, including Jack Daniel's and Southern Comfort. And despite being a company that sells its products in just about every country in the world, descendants of the founder still own more than 70% of it. The company's other whisky brands include Canadian Mist, Early Times, Old Forester and Glenmorangie.

Like many modern multinationals, Brown-Forman's beginnings were relatively modest and required a stroke of profound marketing insight and ingenuity to shape its fortunes. George Garvin Brown, a young pharmaceuticals salesman in Louisville, Kentucky, had what he claimed was the novel idea of selling good whisky in sealed glass bottles, and he founded his company in 1870.

Brown's original brand, Old Forester Kentucky Straight Bourbon, was America's first bottled bourbon. Prior to this bourbon had been sold to taverns in barrels, and bartenders decanted the alcohol into special bottles with the name of the tavern on the label. Brown poured the bourbon into bottles at the distillery, corked and sealed the bottles, labelled them, and warned bars not to buy the bourbon if the seals were broken.

In 1905 Brown-Forman continued its packaging innovations by bottling Old Forester in pear-shaped bottles – it was a huge hit. The company survived Prohibition, which was the downfall of many other distilleries, by being given a licence to sell alcohol for medicinal purposes; then as now, a little of what you fancy clearly does you good.

Currently, the company is involved in a long-running dispute with rival Diageo over a seemingly simple question: when is a whiskey Tennessee whiskey? More than just a war of words, Brown-Forman has become engaged in a war of woods. Under current legislation Tennessee whiskey has to be made not just in the state, but also from at least 51% corn, filtered through maple charcoal and aged in new, charred oak barrels. As it happens, that is the recipe for Jack Daniel's, a whiskey made for more than 100 years that Brown-Forman says continues to be 'made as our fathers made it'.

However, on the other side of this dispute, Diageo is the owner of George Dickel, the brand that is in a distant second place behind Jack Daniel's in the sales rankings of whiskeys produced in Tennessee. Along with some of the state's new wave of distillers, Diageo is lobbying Tennessee politicians to change the rules. These producers argue that they want to be able to mature whiskey in reused barrels, so that they can be free to experiment, and they complain that new barrels are in short supply as the demand for whisky grows worldwide. Diageo adds that not all American whiskey aged in new barrels is of great quality and that there is plenty of outstanding Scotch aged in reused barrels. It says such barrels can be 'rejuvenated' through a process that exposes and chars the wood. So why can they not use old barrels, just like the whisky producers in Scotland?

CAMPARI

The drink Campari begin in Italy in 1860 when Gaspare Campari's experiments culminated in the invention of the famous bitter red aperitif that bears his surname. The drink went on to be a success worldwide, but as a result of industry consolidation in the 1990s it chose a route of international growth by means of acquisition.

In 2009 Campari announced the largest acquisition in its history, buying Wild Turkey, the iconic Kentucky bourbon whiskey, along with American Honey liqueur, a cordial based on honey and bourbon. More recently the company has also bought Canada's Forty Creek Distillery as part of its expansion in North America.

DIAGEO

Diageo is still a relatively young company but it is the largest in the world with a whisky portfolio and some of its brands have a long, rich history. Diageo was created in 1997 through the merger of Grand Metropolitan and Guinness. This created a ragbag of businesses that included a fast-food chain and a maker of donuts, but most of these peripheral activities were sold off so that Diageo could concentrate on alcohol, particularly whisky. Interestingly, the company name has no history in itself and no meaning at all – there is no Mr Diageo and instead the name was created by focus groups.

Its earliest ancestor company, formed in 1749, was Justerini & Brooks, a wine merchant best known for developing the J&B

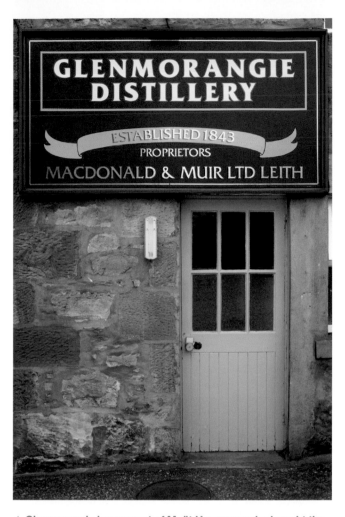

▲ Glenmorangie is now part of Moët Hennessy who bought the company in 2004. (iStock)

▼ In 2014 Bushmills was sold by Diageo, and it is now owned by Mexican giant Jose Cuervo. (Bushmills)

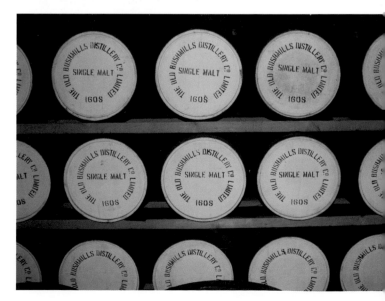

▼ Cragganmore was founded in 1869 and is now part of Diageo.
(Cath Harries)

▲ Lagavulin single malts are renowned for their peaty iodine flavours. (Cath Harries)

◥ Talisker whiskies, from the Isle of Skye, are known for their briny character. (Cath Harries)

◀ Near neighbours on Islay, Caol Ila is owned by Diageo, and Bunnahabhain is part of Burn Stewart Distillers. (Cath Harries)

blended whisky range. In addition Diageo owns Johnnie Walker (the world's most popular blended Scotch whisky), Bell's, White Horse, VAT 69 and Buchanan's (a favourite in Latin America). It has Canada's top whisky (Crown Royal) and – through its Indian company United Distillers – McDowell's (India's top-selling whisky) and Windsor (popular across Asia).

Diageo also has a wide range of single-malt Scotch whiskies, including Caol Ila, Cardhu, Clynelish, Cragganmore, Dalwhinnie, Knockando, Lagavulin and Talisker.

As the whisky industry's expansion continues apace, there is a spring in the step of many of Scotland's distillers, with Diageo at the forefront. The company has stated that it will take its ongoing capital investment in the Highland region alone to almost £150 million, including major expansions at Glen Ord and Teaninich distilleries, and construction of a new distillery at Alness.

HEAVEN HILL

Heaven Hill is America's largest independent, family-owned and operated spirits producer, and the world's second-largest holder of Kentucky bourbon with more than a million barrels stored in its large warehouses, a quantity that accounts for nearly a fifth of the world's unbottled bourbon.

▲ **New oak barrels are an essential component of bourbon.**
(Heaven Hill)

Heaven Hill was founded in 1935 in Bardstown, Kentucky by the Shapira family after the end of Prohibition as a somewhat speculative venture not unlike the 'dot coms' of the 1990s. Its first master distiller was Joseph L. Beam, cousin of Jacob Beam, and all subsequent master distillers have been from the Beam family. The company survived the Second World War by making industrial alcohol, and post-war regular business resumed and prospered.

In 1996 a fire destroyed Heaven Hill's distilling plant in Bardstown. It started in a warehouse and was fuelled by 90,000 barrels of bourbon, witnesses reportedly seeing barrels explode and hurl flames high into the air like rocket trails. The company subsequently purchased the long-established Bernheim distillery in Louisville and has grown ever since, with various acquisitions along the way.

Among Heaven Hill's brands nowadays are Evan Williams (America's second-largest-selling bourbon), Elijah Craig (the original small-batch bourbon) and Old Fitzgerald (a wheated bourbon).

JAGATJIT

Founded in 1944, Jagatjit is India's third-largest producer of spirits. Its whisky range includes Aristocrat Black Whisky, AC Neat Whisky and Old Reserve Whisky. Sold under the 'Spirit of Excellence' banner,

they are a combination of Indian spirits and imported Scotch malts. Recently the company bought a clutch of brands from Scotland's George Sinclair & Sons to help satisfy the growing Indian appetite for Scotch malts.

The company is also the leading producer of Indian Made Foreign Liquor, using grain rather than molasses.

JOHN DISTILLERIES

John Distilleries was established in 1992 by Paul P. John, a first-generation entrepreneur, and has become one of India's leading spirits companies, with a strong portfolio of brands. It is the maker of Original Choice, which is the seventh-largest whisky brand globally and sells 7.8 million cases every year.

In 2012 the company sold its first single-malt whisky, Paul John, a premium single-cask release of only 150 bottles,

◄ **The Evan Williams brand is owned by Heaven Hill.** (Pernod Ricard)

▼ **The fame of Paul John Indian whisky is spread by many tastings worldwide.** (Cath Harries)

▲ **Glenlivet is the number one single malt in the US, and is owned by Pernod Ricard.** (Pernod Ricard)

produced using Indian malted barley and bottled at cask strength. Other releases under the Paul John name have followed.

PERNOD RICARD

The company, the second largest in the world of whisky, can trace its roots back to 1805 when Henri-Louis Pernod founded a distillery in the town of Pontarlier, located in the region of Doubs in eastern France. It made absinthe, a new drink of the time whose recipe Pernod had acquired from its creator, Dr Pierre Ordinaire.

▼ **Sales of the famed, blended Chivas Regal are growing worldwide.** (Chivas Regal)

The Pernod Ricard conglomerate was created in 1975 through the link-up of the Pernod company with another French maker of anise-based spirit called Ricard, which had been founded by Paul Ricard in 1932. The 1980s proved to be an era of corporate expansion through acquisition – and it was often the case that if you did not buy you would be bought. Patrick Ricard, the then boss of Pernod Ricard, had the ambition for his company to conquer first Europe and then the rest of the world.

Pernod Ricard's early acquisitions included Wild Turkey bourbon in 1981 and Irish Distillers – owners of Jameson, Paddy, Powers and Redbreast whiskeys – in 1988. Other wine and spirit companies followed, including the purchase in 2001 of 39.1% of the Canadian company Seagram's wines and spirits business, which included Chivas Regal and Glenlivet whiskies. Pernod Ricard dipped into its large wallet again in 2005 when it bought Allied Domecq, the owner of Ballantine's, in partnership with Fortune Brands. Today, Pernod Ricard owns Royal Stag, one of the most successful whisky brands in India, and is expanding rapidly across Asia.

SAZERAC

The Sazerac Company is a privately owned business that primarily makes bourbon in Kentucky, even though its headquarters is in Metairie, Louisiana. Its operations include the Barton Brands and Buffalo Trace distilleries in Kentucky and the A. Smith Bowman micro-distillery in Virginia.

The company's story starts in New Orleans in a bar known

▼ **Buffalo Trace managed to survive Prohibition by making medicinal whiskey.** Sazerac)

▲ Migrating buffalo gave their name to one of Kentucky's famed bourbon makers. (Sazerac)

as the Sazerac Coffee House, which was bought by Thomas H. Handy in 1869. The Sazerac Coffee House itself was named after a cocktail called the Sazerac that was created in the mid-1800s by a Creole immigrant named Antoine Peychaud, and is often dubbed America's first cocktail – a heady mix of brandy, absinthe and a dash of Peychaud's secret bitters.

To make cocktails, spirits are needed and Handy went on to buy several spirits companies. Except for a stint as a delicatessen and grocery vendor during Prohibition, the company has been involved in spirits ever since.

▼ Good bourbon takes time to make and so deserves thoughtful contemplation. (Sazerac)

THE WORLD'S TOP 10 WHISKIES

	Brand	Owner	Category
1	McDowell's No 1	United Spirits	Indian
2	Johnnie Walker	Diageo	Scotch
3	Officer's Choice	Allied Blenders & Distillers	Indian
4	Bagpiper	United Spirits	Indian
5	Royal Stag	Pernod Ricard	Indian
6	Old Tavern	United Spirits	Indian
7	Original Choice	John Distillers	Indian
8	Jack Daniel's	Brown-Forman	US (Tennessee)
9	Imperial Blue	Pernod Ricard	Indian
10	Haywards	United Spirits	Indian

THE WORLD'S TOP 10 SCOTCH WHISKIES

	Brand	Owner
1	Johnnie Walker	Diageo
2	Ballantine's	Pernod Ricard
3	Chivas Regal	Pernod Ricard
4	J&B Rare	Diageo
5	William Grant's	William Grant & Son
6	The Famous Grouse	Erdington
7	Dewar's	Bacardi
8	William Lawson's	Bacardi
9	Label 5	La Martiniquaise
10	Bell's	Diageo

NORTH AMERICAN TOP 10

	Brand	Owner
1	Jack Daniel's	Brown-Forman
2	Jim Beam	Beam Suntory
3	Crown Royal	Diageo
4	Seagram's 7 Crown	Diageo
5	Black Velvet	Constellation Brands
6	Canadian Club	Beam Suntory
7	Canadian Mist	Brown-Forman
8	Evan Williams	Heaven Hill
9	Wild Turkey	Campari
10	Maker's Mark	Beam Suntory

Source: *Drinks International*, 2013

Whisky around the world

Whisky is produced in various guises all over the world and not just in Scotland, as some people think. Japanese whisky, Irish whiskey and American whiskey are all winning plaudits and accolades, while India has become a major producer.

Today, whiskies are produced in more than 30 countries. This section looks at the major whisky-producing nations and an intriguing cross-section of the unexpected ones.

SCOTLAND

Scotland has the greatest concentration of distilleries in the world and is rightly regarded as the spiritual home of whisky, even though the Irish might argue against this. With more than 100 active distilleries, Scottish whiskies are among the world's most revered spirits and they offer astonishing diversity. Some of Scotland's distilleries survive from a period of extraordinary activity 150 years ago, when whisky started to strut on a world stage, while others are new, high-tech distilleries that are proud to use up-to-date, environmentally sensitive technology.

Single-malt Scotch whiskies can be divided into six geographical groups. Five of the regions are recognised by the Scotch Whisky Association, but one, Island, is not. While some might say there are distinct regional styles, it is unwise to make broad generalisations.

Highland and Lowland whisky-producing areas originally had different tax regimes. The Wash Act of 1784 established a precise geographical Highland Line that separated the Lowlands from the Highlands for the purposes of differential excise levels, as well as considerably reducing the level of

duty and simplifying regulations. The aim of the Act was to stimulate legal distilling in the Highlands and to reduce illicit distilling. As with most tax legislation, there were winners and losers. Lower rates of duty were applied to small-scale distilleries north of the line and stills were regulated in size to a maximum of 30 gallons. According to the law, only one still per distillery was allowed, only grain grown within the parish could be used, and the whisky made had to be consumed locally.

One unintended consequence of the legislation was that Ferintosh distillery, probably Scotland's oldest distillery, the location of which can still be recognised, lost the right – granted in 1689 – to distil free of duty, leading to the distillery having to shut in 1785 because the owner could not afford to pay his tax bill.

Highland

North of the line from the River Tay in the east to the River Clyde in the west, the Highlands form the biggest whisky region. Remote and sparsely populated, this region once had many distillers operating illicit stills.

Single-malt whiskies from the Highlands come in many complexions. In the north, some are big, with cereal sweetness as exhibited by Dalmore. Head south and the whiskies tend to be fruitier, with a slaking dryness such as Aberfeldy. In the east there are full-bodied, dry whiskies with

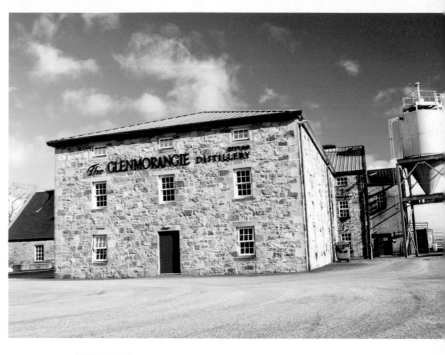

◀ India's Amrut distillery was established in 1948, in Bangalore. (Amrut)

▲ At the Speyside Aberlour distillery, visitors can fill their own bottle as part of a tour. (Pernod Ricard)

▶ The Glenmorangie distillery is rightly regarded as one of Scotland's top whisky attractions. (iStock)

lots of fruit and aromatic swirls such as Glen Garioch. Go west and many of the whiskies are full-bodied with peaty, smoky overtones, and nearer the coast there are some more salty, seaweed-flavoured whiskies.

▼ Glenmorangie's still room is one of the most magnificent in the whole of Scotland. (iStock)

Speyside

Speyside distilleries are located in the valley of the River Spey. Although the region falls within the Highlands, its concentration of distilleries is deemed to require it to be a separate region and it is home to the majority of Scotland's distilleries.

Generally Speyside malts tend to be lighter and sweeter than others, and the area is also renowned for the quality

▲ **Lagavulin's coastal location is said to influence the character of its whisky.** (Cath Harries)

of the barley grown there. The Glenlivet and Glenfiddich distilleries produce the most classic, typical Speyside drams, and both are world-famous. However, a group of distilleries does produce heavily sherried-style whiskies, with Glenfarclas and The Macallan, for example, producing big-bodied flavours.

Islay

Islay malts come from the island of Islay, which is generally associated with heavily peated and medicinally flavoured malts. They are not to everyone's taste, but single-malt whiskies such as Ardbeg, Bowmore, Laphroaig and Lagavulin are all world-renowned and for any whisky traveller a visit to Islay is a 'must'.

The island is also home to such stars as Bunnahabhain, Bruichladdich, Caol Ila and the up-and-coming Kilchoman, all of which are fruitier, less peaty drams.

Island

The Islands represent a very diverse region and one that is not strictly recognised as a region by the Scotch Whisky Association – technically the Islands are a part of the Highlands.

On Orkney can be found Highland Park and Scapa. From the Isle of Skye comes Talisker. The Isle of Arran has its own rich malt. On Mull the Tobermory distillery produces a sweet, thick, slightly herbal whisky and a heavily peated version called Ledaig, while on the Isle of Jura the eponymous distillery produces some slightly maritime, oily drams with a nutty cereal character.

▼ **Scapa may be an island distillery, but its Orkney whiskies are anything but peaty.** (Pernod Ricard)

▼ **Winter is harsh on Jura, but that doesn't stop palms growing within sight of the distillery.** (Cath Harries)

▲ Deanston Highland whiskies are noted for fruity and estery flavours. (Pernod Ricard)

▼ The Springbank distillery is the last distillery in Campbeltown – once there were 20. (Cath Harries)

Lowland

Lowland malts come from south of that imaginary line from the River Tay in the east to the River Clyde in the west. It is probably home to the most 'lost souls' – Scotland's closed distilleries. Because the region has so few distilleries, nowadays it is often lumped together with Campbeltown.

Traditionally this region's whiskies were known for their soft, floral characteristics and its single-malt distilleries have earned the nickname 'Lowland Ladies' – fiery drams come from elsewhere! It is probably the predominance of continuous column stills that give the region's whiskies their soft subtleties. Auchentoshan is the last of the region's distillers to use triple distillation.

Campbeltown

Campbeltown malts come from Argyll on the Mull of Kintyre. The region used to be the most prolific in Scotland and once had more than 20 distilleries. The malts are noted for their dryness, with some coastal characteristics. Longrow, which is produced at the Springbank distillery, has some peaty characteristics.

IRELAND

A century ago Prohibition in the US and the war of independence within Ireland all but finished the Irish whiskey industry – a swift decline for what was once the world's biggest distilling nation. But the industry picked itself up by the boot straps, having been all but abandoned by customers in the USA, and today there is renewed positivity about making whiskey on the island and several new distillers are drawing up plans to start production and open visitor centres.

◀ Jameson whiskey is particularly popular in America.
(Jameson)

The Emerald Isle is renowned for its triple-distilled whiskey blends such as Jameson and the more scarce single pot-still whiskeys as exemplified by brands such as Redbreast and Green Spot, but most Irish whiskey is made using continuous stills.

Until recently there were only four operating distilleries in Ireland, all owned by multinational companies: Kilbeggan in County Westmeath (owned by Suntory), Cooley in County Louth (Suntory), Bushmills in County Antrim (Jose Cuervo) and Midleton in County Cork (Pernod Ricard). Today, however, new distilleries are being opened across the country.

The Bushmills distillery has the world's oldest distillery licence, issued in 1608, but Bushmills itself did not come into existence until 1743, when whisky chronicler Alfred Barnard recorded it as having been in the hands of smugglers.

Even though Ireland has a great deal of peat, it is unusual to find an Irish whiskey with the smoky, peaty notes found in Islay whiskies.

UNITED STATES

The production of American whiskey, be it bourbon or Tennessee, became focused on Kentucky and Tennessee. Prohibition, however, cast a long shadow over the US and most of the country's distillers closed down, many of the styles of whiskey they produced disappearing with them. This opened the market to imports that have dominated the market for the best part of eight decades.

Imported spirit was seen as sophisticated, while home-produced distilled grain drinks were for blue-collar workers. How times change. A revolution has swept the US – similar to its beer transformation – and today there are hundreds of local distillers.

Bourbon is still the most common style and has to be made from 51% corn and matured in virgin oak barrels. But times are changing and there is a new wave of distillers wanting to make imaginative drinks using locally grown grains. Rye is making a comeback in north-eastern states, moonshine is being made legally, and several brewers are experimenting by distilling some of their beers.

However, as many roads in Scotland take whisky fans to Islay, it is hard to ignore the new producers in Kentucky who are making exciting whiskeys in some dynamic styles. Distillers are rediscovering moonshine, rye, wheat, corn and the influence of different woods – the rule book is being torn up.

CANADA

Canada has been making distilled spirits for over two centuries. The first Canadian distillery was opened in Quebec City in 1769, and by the 1840s there were over 200 distilleries in the country. Canada had its own Prohibition era too, from 1916 to 1917.

By definition Canadian whiskies – often referred to as rye whiskies – are grain spirits that have been aged in charred oak barrels for a minimum of three years. In 1875 the Canadian government specified that Canadian whisky must be distilled in multiple column stills and aged in unused or used oak, in Canada, for at least three years. Canadian whisky uses different combinations of rye, barley, corn and wheat, and ageing is in barrels of new oak or those previously used for bourbon, sherry or brandy.

The style is very similar to Scotch blended whisky, save for the oft-used rye. One of Canada's whisky pioneers was Hiram Walker, who established his distillery in Detroit in 1858 and later moved it to Ontario, Canada, where he founded Walkerville, his own town. Hiram Walker created the brand Canadian Club, which has become globally popular. Such was Walker's success that he established two whisky distilleries in Scotland.

◀ Bottling bourbon at the Buffalo Trace distillery in Kentucky.
(Sazerac)

▲ Japanese whisky has rightly won plaudits worldwide.
(Cath Harries)

▲ Yamazaki's wash ferments for up to three days before heading to the stills. (Beam Suntory)

▼ Three large stills dominate Yamazaki's elegant still room .
(Beam Suntory)

JAPAN

One of the fastest-growing whisky countries, Japan draws on Scotland for its inspiration. Shinjiro Torii and Masataka Taketsuru are regarded as the founders of the industry in the land of the rising sun.

Torii, a saki brewer and shopkeeper, established the Suntory brand and in 1923 founded the first Japanese whisky distillery – Yamazaki in the Vale of Yamazaki. Before the First World War he had stored alcohol for liqueurs in old wine barrels and ended up forgetting about them. Some years later he tried the liquid to check what it was, and discovered that ageing in barrels had profoundly enriched the flavour. This convinced him that he could make his own whisky.

Taketsuru studied briefly at the University of Glasgow in

▼ Opened in 1923, Yamazaki was Japan first whisky distillery.
(Beam Suntory)

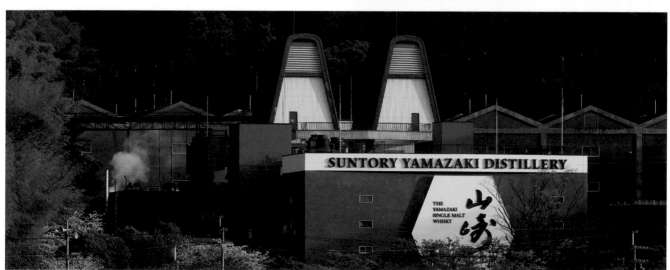

SUNTORY YAMAZAKI DISTILLERY

▲ **India has become known as a whisky making country thanks to Amrut.** (Amrut)

▼ **According to Indian legend, the elixir of life, called Amrut, sprang out from the ground near the distillery.** (Amrut)

1919 and for a while worked in Scotland at the Longmorn, Ben Nevis and Hazelburn distilleries. After he returned to Japan in 1920 with his new Scottish wife, Rita, he built Yoichi distillery on the northerly island of Hokkaido in an area that he believed to be similar to Scotland.

The sweet floral notes often associated with Japanese whisky probably come from the slow-growing Japanese oak from which the barrels are made. Japanese whiskies are made in a range of styles and there is a wide variety of ages. Each distillery tries to make every possible whisky style using many malt types and wood-maturing styles, involving different woods, new and used.

Some blended Japanese whisky is a mixture of both malt and grain spirit, often containing a percentage of imported Scottish malt. Blended Japanese whiskies use expressions from the same distillery.

INDIA

India is the world's largest producer of whisky. Many Indian whiskies, however, would be more appropriately described as rum because they are made from molasses, but the country's labelling regulations are sufficiently loose that these spirits can be described as whisky. Molasses comes from sugar cane, which is widely grown in India. Most of the molasses-based drinks are sold on the domestic market.

Some Indian whisky even gets blended with imported whisky; in addition a proportion is distilled in continuous stills using buckwheat, rice and millet; and it is often sold unaged.

Growing amounts of distillates, however, are crafted, distilled and matured to meet regulations governing Scotch single-malt whisky. Probably the best-known such distillery is Amrut, which was established in 1948 in Bangalore, in the heart of southern India, and exports most of its production. Forty years later McDowell's distillery in Goa began malt whisky production.

India's climate means maturation occurs much more quickly than in colder climes, so even the older Indian whiskies tend to be quite young. The temperature is such that 'the angels' share' – the proportion of a whisky's volume that is lost to evaporation during ageing – is around 12% alcohol by volume per annum.

REST OF THE WORLD

From Argentina to Wales, more than 30 countries now make whisky and many follow what has become the Holy Trinity of a distillation made from malted barley, water and yeast, and stored in oak for three years. However, there is also a brave new world where new whisky-producing countries – as well as some traditional ones – are ripping up the rule book and turning to local ingredients and woods. The world of whisky has never been so exciting!

Argentina

Whisky distilling in Argentina is small and yet to be perfectly formed. La Alazana in the Patagonia region was the first to produce a commercial expression. Established in 2011 by Néstor Serenelli and Pablo Tognetti, it is producing a single-malt whisky that has been aged in American bourbon oak casks and Argentinian sherry casks.

Australia

Distilling was banned in Australia for almost 150 years until the law was rescinded in 1992 but now the country has 18 distilleries, ten of them in Tasmania. If this nascent industry becomes as successful as the country's wine production, within a few years it will make its mark on the world stage. The warm climate helps the whisky to mature more quickly than in more temperate climates.

At Lark Distillery, Tasmania's first distillery set up by Bill Lark in 1992, the distillers have developed a technique for smoking grain after it has been malted. Sullivans Cove is another Tasmanian distiller gaining plaudits, with its expressions winning awards worldwide. Another to watch is Bakery Hill, founded in 1998 in the state of Victoria.

Austria

Austria now has at least 15 producers of whisky – not bad for a country that did not start to make whisky until 1995 and until then was better known for its fruit-based brandies.

The first Austrian distillery was Haider, in the Waldviertel. In addition to single-malts, it produces some rye whiskies, while spelt and corn are also mashed; several of its products are flavoured with peat smoke. All Haider's whiskies are sold at cask strength to emphasise their strong flavours as much as possible. About 70,000 litres of whisky is stored at Haider and the distillery is experimenting with storing spirit in sweet wine casks. The distillery has a famed visitor centre.

▲ **Two redundant Scottish pot stills found a new home at Het Ankers in Belgium.** (Het Ankers)

Belgium

As Belgium has a rich tradition of making beer, it is somewhat surprising that the country has lacked a tradition of making whisky.

The Belgian Owl Distillery led the way and was commissioned in 2004. The Het Anker brewery bought a couple of pot stills from the Forsyth distillery in Scotland to distil its Gouden Carolus beer to a single-malt whisky. It is put into bourbon casks for two and a half years before going into Het Anker barrels for a further six months.

Since 2006 the brewer Duvel has been at work on a

▼ **Duvel in Belgium is a world famed brewer which has started to make its own beer-based spirit.** (Duvel)

crossover product combining Belgian brewing and distilling. The brewery had a batch of Duvel beer distilled, a process that took 90 days, and then aged it for six years in oak bourbon and sherry barrels. As yet Duvel is not calling the product whisky.

Brazil

Brazilians buy a great deal of imported whisky, but they do not make much themselves. The Union Distillery was founded in 1948 and has been making a sought-after single-malt whisky since the 1970s. Built in the 1960s, Busnello Distillery is located in a castle and makes blended and single-malt expressions that are matured for eight years in oak casks.

▲ Visitors to Adnams' still room in Southwold, Suffolk, have a fabulous view of the town's lighthouse. (Anthony Cullen)

▼ Most distilleries which offer visitor tours, like Adnams, have a shop where whisky can be bought. (Cath Harries)

Corsica

From the island of Corsica, P&M Whiskies represents the joint efforts of two local businesses, Pietra (a brewery) and Domaine Mavela (a producer of liqueurs and other spirits), who together have been producing a whisky since 2001. The spirit ages for at least three years in 100-year-old oak casks that previously held Muscat wine.

Czech Republic

In 1989 the Pradlo Distillery in western Czechoslovakia began a project to create a single-malt whisky. Using only Czech barley and the crisp, clean water of the Bohemia region, this whisky was aged for over 20 years in casks made of 100% Czech oak. Named Hammer Head, the name is derived from the milling machine that crushes the Czech malt.

Another distiller is Jelinek, which makes the blended whiskies Gold Cock and Red Feathers.

Denmark

Denmark could soon become a powerhouse for craft distilling. At least six distilleries are now in operation and several more are expected to open soon.

The first Danish single-malt was produced by Lille Gadegård in 2005. The Stauning distillery, near Skjern, has been winning many plaudits for its rye expressions, some of which are smoked. Also worth seeking out is the Bryghuset Braunstein, which was set up in 2007; it produces one peated and one unpeated whisky each year, and the expressions are stored in first-fill oak barrels.

England

England is now a whisky country, production having returned after a 100-year absence. Leading the way is St George's in Norfolk, while famed brewer Adnams now has its own distillery. Cornwall is home to Hicks & Healey, which gets its wash from the St Austell brewery. In Cumbria the Lakes Distillery makes an interesting British blend. The London Distillery Company is now operating but it will be some years before its expressions go on sale. And the Cotswold Distillery and the Oxford Artisan Distillery are expected to be operational soon.

Finland

In a country with some of the world's most restrictive rules concerning alcohol, it has not been easy for distillers to set up. The first commercially available whisky from Finland is produced by the Teerenpeli distillery, which was founded in 2002 in Lahti and is based in a brewery. Panimoravintola Beer Hunters is a small producer that has been winning a lot of praise from aficionados; its whiskies are aged in used sherry casks.

▶ **Brittany's Glann ar Mor distillery produces
a smoky single-malt.** (Glann ar Mor)

France

France has a long history of distillation,
but it is only in the past 20–30
years that distillers have turned
their undoubted skills to making
whiskies. At Glann ar Mor in Brittany
the owners have two small direct-
fired stills and one of this distillery's
expressions is made with local,
smoky peat. Warenghem, also in
Brittany, has turned to grain after
100 years of making fruit distillations.
The Menhirs distillery has been
experimenting with a distillate made
from buckwheat.

Germany

Germany has a long tradition of distilling fruit brandies,
schnapps and herbal concoctions, but it is relatively new
to the world of whisky. There are a dozen or so companies
making whisky, mostly in relatively small quantities.

Bavarian distillery Slyrs opened in 1999 and has released its
first 12-year-old expression; Bavarian malt is used and the spirit
is stored in American white oak barrels. Blaue Maus distillery was
established in 1980, but it was three years before it started to
make a whisky and its older expressions have won rave reviews.
Since 2007 Alpirsbacher Brauwelt has been making a single-
malt spirit that is stored in lightly charred German oak barrels.

Italy

January 2010 saw the opening of Italy's first whisky distillery,
Puni, high up in the Alps in the Ortler mountain range. Its two pot
stills were made in Rothes, Scotland, its malt is locally grown,
and its oak barrels are stored in former Second World War
military bunkers that get very warm in summer, causing relatively
fast maturation. Puni's single-malt whisky comprises three
types of malt – barley, wheat and rye. It uses a range of barrels
including bourbon barrels from the United States, marsala casks
from Sicily and pinot noir wine casks from South Tyrol.

Liechtenstein

Although the Tesler distillery was established in 1880, it
has only started to distil whisky in recent years, under the
management of the fourth generation of the founding family.
The still is fired over an open wood fire, the wash is given a
long conditioning period to fully ferment, and the whisky is
matured in former pinot noir casks.

▶ **German brewer Alpirsbacher produces a malt-based spirit
from this curious looking still.** (Alpirsbacher)

Netherlands

The Dutch make a great deal of gin but until recently they
have not turned their obvious distilling skills to whisky. Zuidam
Distillery, which is better known for its Dutch genevers, produces
the Millstone single-malt range, which has certainly created
interest as a result of their experimentation with different woods
and grains, peated and unpeated. The Us Heit distillery in
Bolsward makes a single-malt called Frysk Hynder; each barrel,
when bottled, has its own character and unique taste.

New Zealand

Given the close links to Scotland, perhaps more distilleries
would be expected in New Zealand, but government pressure
drove most out of business by the 1870s.

Willowbank Distillery was opened by the Baker family in
1974 but stopped production in 1997. The old stock was
bought and is now being released to much acclaim. New
Zealand Double Wood whisky is aged for 15 years in both
American oak and French pinot noir barrels.

Norway

The much-acclaimed brand Agder Brenneri released the
first true Norwegian whisky, Audny, in 2012, the company's

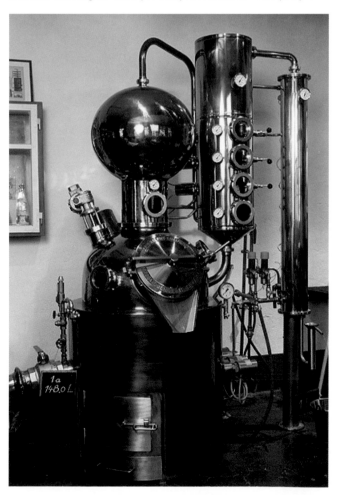

whiskies prior to that date having been blends of Scottish malts. The change began in 2005 when Agder Brenneri managed to break the 80-year-old Norwegian state monopoly on spirit production and their first whisky expressions were matured in sherry casks.

The Aass Brewery has also made its own whisky. The base of the drink was a batch of its Christmas beer, which was then distilled and aged in oak barrels. As this drink contains hops, strictly speaking it cannot be called whisky and is therefore labelled 'eau de vie de bière'.

A group of Norwegian whisky enthusiasts launched the world's first Arctic whisky! Myken whisky is distilled in an old fish factory on the island of Myken off the north coast of Norway.

Pakistan

The British civil service brought brewing and distilling to Pakistan in the 1860s, and 100 years later the Murree brewery and distillery started making whisky in earnest, storing it in oak casks imported from the US, Australia and Spain. The distillery states that it has over 500,000 casks maturing in its large underground warehouse.

Russia

Russia has imported whisky rather than make it, as the country's distillers prefer to stick to producing vodka. However, Vladimir Malashenko, brewer at the Munhell brewery in St Petersburg, is experimenting with a distillation that will be stored in new oak barrels. Currently the project is at research stage but he hopes it will become commercial one day.

South Africa

James Sedgwick Distillery, situated at the foot of the Limietberg Mountains in Wellington, is home of the award-winning range of Three Ships whiskies. It makes both malt and grain whiskies and has more than 70,000 casks maturing.

Draymans is a brewer turned distiller. Its Solera whisky is a blend of Scotch and South African whiskies that is then further cask-matured using the 'solera' process, which sees fractions of the contents of the oldest barrels combined with pulls from newer barrels; as spirit is removed from the oldest barrel, it is replaced with wine from the second-oldest barrel, and so on.

Spain

Spain's whisky of choice is DYC, now part of the Beam Suntory empire. Its best-selling variety is its four-year blended expression, which is matured in American oak barrels from the Beam bourbon distillery, but an eight-year-old whisky is also produced and in 2009 there was also a ten-year-old single-malt to commemorate DYC's 50th anniversary.

A new kid on the block in Spain is Liber distillery, which was founded in 2001, at first to make gin and vodka, but nowadays it sells a five-year-old single-malt whisky called Embrujo de Granada.

González Byass, the sherry maker, is also new to whisky as it started marketing the aptly named Nomad in 2014. This is a blended whisky produced in Scotland but aged in Spain: it is sourced from Speyside – blended from around 30 single-malt and grain whiskies aged between five and eight years – and shipped to Jerez in southern Spain to be aged in Pedro Ximénez barrels.

Sweden

Sweden now has 13 whisky distilleries, all founded since 2002.

Mackmyra is the oldest of them and is named after its home village, not a mythical Scottish glen! The whisky is matured in three kinds of barrels: used Jack Daniel's bourbon barrels, used sherry casks from Spain, and brand new oak barrels. Its peated malt is smoked with local peat, which contains juniper – which imparts a fragrant aromatic kick.

The Box distillery was founded in 2007 and its first bottlings have been greeted with huge acclaim. Located on the island of Öland, Wannborga is Sweden's smallest distillery and states that it makes whisky 'mainly for fun'.

Switzerland

Switzerland has at least ten distillers, all of which have emerged since 1999, when the law was changed to allow the distillation of grain in addition to the country's long tradition of distilling fruit. As in Scotland, regulations require Swiss single-malt whiskies to be matured in barrels for at least three years.

The Bader family made the country's first whisky, Holle single-malt, which is characterised by notes of honey and caramelised apples, and aged in Burgundy wine barrels that have been used for both red and white wine. Brauerei Locher, Switzerland's largest independent brewery, makes Appenzeller Säntis Malt using barley and grains grown in Switzerland's mountain areas. At Whisky Castle distillery, spirit is matured in chestnut and oak barrels, with some expressions made from beech-smoked barley malt.

Taiwan

The first bottle of Kavalan was released in December 2008 and it is now the best-selling Taiwanese whisky. Kavalan, which means 'flatland people', is named after the Taiwanese aboriginal ethnic group that originally inhabited modern-day Yilan County, home to the distillery. The warm subtropical climate of Taiwan ensures that the whiskies mature faster than their Scottish, American and Japanese counterparts. Ex-sherry, port and bourbon barrels are used for ageing and all this distillery's products are cask strength, non-chill filtered and natural in colour.

Ukraine

When it comes to spirits, most Ukrainians prefer vodka or brandy. However, Ukraine's oldest brewery in the western region of the ancient town of Mykulyntsi is birthplace to

▲ **Coopers' tools are on display at the Penderyn distillery in Wales.** (Cath Harries)

the country's first home-produced whisky, Mykulynetska, which is characterised by a deep amber/gold colour and a soft, silky texture.

Wales

Wales might only have one distillery, Penderyn in the foothills of the Brecon Beacons, but its single-malt whisky, launched in 2004, has quickly made a mark on the world stage with its aromatic expressions. A quarter of its production is exported, with France being its largest overseas market. Penderyn's success means that its wash is now made in-house, rather than at the Brains brewery in Cardiff.

▶ **Penderyn's range of whiskies can be sampled after a distillery tour.** (Cath Harries)

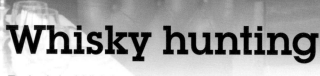

(all *Whisky hunting* photos Cath Harries)

Whisky hunting

Boisdale Whisky Bar in Canary Wharf, in the Docklands area of east London, is rightly regarded as one of the top whisky bars in the world. The man who runs this theatre of drams, the mad maestro orchestrating the spirits and bringing them to life, is bar manager Ernest Reid.

There is something endearingly eccentric about the Boisdale. Scottish food, whisky and great jazz – all are part of its magic. There is a Scottish theme to most of the food on the menu, which includes Loch Ryan native oysters (when in season), organic Hebridean salmon and Aberdeenshire beef sirloin.

Whisky is the drink of choice for many of the bar's customers and few fail to be entranced by the large and idiosyncratic range on offer. Here whisky is honoured and revered as the finest Bordeaux wines would be in France.

Ordering a whisky from the Glenfarclas Family Cask, c1957, is not for the faint-hearted. A 50ml measure will set you back £220. According to staff, it is a very rich, dark whisky, which reflects almost no light through the bottle. It is supposed to be full of sherry, coffee and stewed fruit flavours and after it has been exposed to the air some sense macadamia nuts. However, there is a large range of good whiskies at more affordable prices.

Ernest Reid is the curator of more than 700 bottles of single malts and other whiskies from around the world. The bottles – some very old and rare – stand on high shelves behind the bar and Ernest seems to know every one as an old friend. In fact nothing seems to please him more than having the chance to move effortlessly up and down the shelves choosing bottles of liquid history.

'Some of these whiskies have been in a barrel longer than I've been alive,' says Ernest. 'You have to build yourself up slowly to taste some of them. It's right to respect them and give them time.'

'I think of each as a different style of music when I choose one to drink. What do I want? Drum and bass or pop? Rock and roll or something jazzy? Here at Boisdale there is a whisky for everyone.'

Here is a selection of star bottles at this cathedral of celebrated cereal distillations.

1 This is an early example of the blended White Horse whisky, a drink that first rose to prominence among passengers travelling on the eight-day stagecoach journey from Edinburgh to London. The brand has a long history, stretching back to the late 19th century, and is named after the White Horse Cellar Inn that still stands in Edinburgh's Canongate.

2 Only 723 bottles of the legendary White Bowmore 1964 were ever produced. It was matured in bourbon casks for 43 years in Bowmore's famed No 1 vault. It is infused with light, luscious vanilla tones and has a very subtle golden hue. At a recent auction a bottle sold for over £5,000.

3 The Black Bowmore was distilled on 5 November 1964 and was the first instalment of the Bowmore 1964 'Trilogy'. The spirit spent four decades maturing in Oloroso sherry casks and only 827 bottles of it were produced.

4 Even rarer is a Macallan 1946, which, unusually for the Speyside distillery, was made with peated malt as the price of coal was high at the time, just after the war. It has swirling, smoky aromas and flavours with hints of ginger spices and apple fruits.

5 A little younger but almost as distinguished is a Macallan 1971, which matured for 30 years in the same first-fill sherry cask – filled on 3 May 1971 – and is one of only 536 bottles produced. The nose and taste are full of mixed dried fruits and wood spices.

6 Pappy Van Winkle's Family Reserve is a limited-edition, 23-year-old bourbon that is best enjoyed neat. All of the Van Winkle bourbons are made in Kentucky with corn, wheat and barley, the use of wheat rather than rye giving this whiskey a smoother taste. Since 2002 Van Winkle's bourbons have been distilled and bottled by the Sazerac Company at its Buffalo Trace Distillery in Frankfort, prior to which the bourbon was made at the Stitzel-Weller Distillery in Louisville.

7 Two royal weddings are commemorated at Boisdale. Released in 1981, the Macallan Royal Marriage sees the joining together of casks from 1948 and 1961, the birth years of Prince Charles and Lady Diana; a Speyside malt, this has the characteristic notes of spirit matured in ex-sherry casks from

7

Jerez. A porcelain decanter from Bell's was bottled to celebrate the marriage of Prince Andrew and Sarah Ferguson in 1986. While distillers love to celebrate weddings, no expressions have been released to mark the couples' divorces.

8 Many whisky books say that all Scotch whisky is double-distilled, but this is not true. One of the most renowned triple-distilled malts is Hazelburn, an unpeated malt made just like an Irish whiskey at the Springbank distillery in Campbeltown, a small town west of Glasgow that once had 34 distilleries and proclaimed itself the whisky capital of the world – but after pride came the fall and today only three distilleries exist. This eight-year-old is a cask-strength edition of Hazelburn, which was bottled for the Springbank Society in 2006.

6　　**7**　　**8**　　**9**

9 Cereal chic met punk in 2011 when a Chivas Regal 18 range was styled by the fashion designer Vivienne Westwood to mark her 70th birthday. She wrapped the bottle with a folded silk flag based on a 19th-century flag design.

10 A trio of St Magdalene malts, aged 17, 19 and 26 years. This Lowland distillery was established during the late 18th century by Sebastian Henderson but closed in 1983, so it is now a 'silent distillery'. Its bottlings are described as being as rare as hens' teeth: only 6,000 bottles were released of the 19-year-old St Magdalene, which was casked in 1979 and bottled in 1998.

11 Only eight carefully chosen refill casks make up the exceptional

character of the Highland Park 1968, which saw an initial release of 1,550 bottles in 2009. Fans are clamouring for more of this Orkney whisky, which has honey and lemongrass flavours.

12 Orkney is also home to one of Scotland's silent distilleries, which was mothballed by its owners in 1994. The Scapa distillery was established in 1885 by Glasgow distillers Townsend & MacFarlane and for most of its life it produced whisky for use in blends such as Teacher's and Ballantine's, but a few official bottlings of Scapa single-malt were released. One such is part of a limited release of 2,000 bottles of Scapa, which was distilled in 1980 and aged for 25 years before bottling at cask strength. It is a big, bold whisky, full of spicy flavours and notes of honey and Christmas pudding spices and fruits.

13 Another rarity is The Balvenie 1973, which was distilled on 21 May 1973 and bottled on 28 April 2004, a few days shy of its 31st birthday. According to the distillery only 309 bottles were produced, all from cask number 7484, and the bottle at Boisdale is number 263. Full of ginger and lemongrass flavours, it has a finish as long as Boisdale's bar.

14 The Glenrothes 1972 and 1979 are regarded as two of the best whiskies ever made. The Speyside distillery is famed for the quality of its whiskies, which frequently underpin some of the world's finest blends, such as Cutty Sark, and its single-malt releases are both rare and finite.

15 There cannot be many bottles of Glenmorangie's 1963 left in the world. This Scotch was bottled in 1987, having been stored in oak bourbon casks before spending the last two years of its maturation in Spanish Oloroso sherry casks. For some reason 50 bottles of it sat unnoticed for many years in Glenmorangie's warehouse until their discovery by master distiller Bill Lumsden. This treasure trove, a time capsule from the year President Kennedy was assassinated, was then rebottled and all the bottles were sold for charity. This is a whisky that has been given time and anyone sipping it should give it time too in order to relish its balance of oak spice and sherry sweetness.

The Glenmorangie 1991 and 1993 are other examples of this distillery's experimentation with different woods. The Glenmorangie 1991, bottled in 2002, was matured in American new oak from Missouri to give it a bourbon tang and only 1,000 bottles of it were ever released. The Glenmorangie 1993 was matured in casks of new burr oak, another variety of American oak; full of fruit and spice flavours, it is warming with lingering hints of cinnamon spice and orange.

16 The Ardbeg distillery is located in a remote spot on the south-east coast of Islay. This is a distillery that has come back from the dead: after being mothballed for the period 1982–89 it is now producing some of the world's most distinctive and renowned whiskies. Boisdale's collection of its heavily peated whiskies, some of which are flavoured with distinctive phenolics, contains some expressions that cannot be found in the distillery any more. Much sought-after are the whiskies that form the Ardbeg Committee: these limited-edition expressions are produced annually for members of the Ardberg fan club and offer an exploration into how whisky changes over time in a barrel.

16

◀ **Whisky dreams come true in the best whisky stores.**
(Cath Harries)

▶ **Duncan Ross and his colleagues are there to guide customers to their favourite drams.** (Cath Harries)

The lost distilleries

One of the best places to go for advice on buying whisky, whether for personal consumption or investment, has to be the Whisky Exchange on London's South Bank. Here can be found some of the world's really rare bottles – the products of Scotland's 'lost distilleries'.

Duncan Ross and his colleagues at the Whisky Exchange must be some of the most knowledgeable and friendly whisky experts on the planet. Their shop sells more than 1,000 single-malt whiskies – and that is only the start of its range of whiskies.

Standing on shelves next to whiskies from just about every significant producer in the world are some of the world's most scarce bottles. Here can be seen bottles from some of Scotland's lost distilleries – bottles that are much sought-after by collectors. Indeed it is not uncommon, says Duncan, for people to contact the Whisky Exchange saying that they have found an unopened bottle of whisky at the back of an old cupboard and wanting to know if it is worth anything.

One reason why rarity occurs is because whisky production has always been something of a rollercoaster. At its height towards the end of the 19th century there were more than 200 distilleries in Scotland, but by the end of the Second World War at least 70 of these had closed. Then there was something of a renaissance as production increased in most years until 1980, but then came a drop in sales and a consequent glut of whisky, resulting in the closure of many distilleries during the ensuing decade.

'Until the late 1980s most of the whisky being sold around the world was blended Scotch,' states Duncan. 'Single-malts were not really important and were very small in terms of volume sales.'

When a decision was made to shut down a distillery, therefore, it was usually one that was small, remote, inefficient and knackered – and one that probably contributed little to the

balance of a blend. However, since then many whisky drinkers have started to seek out single-malts in their quest for the perfect dram.

'It was Diageo that was first to realise the importance of limited-edition issues of single-malts, often from closed

▼ **The Elements of Islay range showcases the best of the island's whisky creations.** (Cath Harries)

◀ **Many drinkers now seek out cask-strength whisky.**
(Cath Harries)

distilleries,' continues Duncan. 'Diageo's limited releases were targeted at serious whisky fans, and they often experimented with different wood finishes.'

These limited editions have become much sought-after by collectors. Currently there is stock available from around 30 lost distilleries, and the price for most of these increases with every new release.

However, Duncan cautions, information on how much whisky is available from lost distilleries is elusive, with distillers and bottlers keeping it very close to their chests. As a rule of thumb, he says, price is the main clue: if a release from a lost distillery costs considerably more than previous releases, this is a pretty good indication that stock could be running out. He cites the case of Kinclaith, which could be bought for £30 a bottle 15 years ago. Then the bottler, Gordon & Macphail, ran out of stock and the price quickly increased to £500 a bottle. And now it is available again, but rarely at less than £700 a bottle.

Strange to think that some of the most collectible whiskies were originally discarded because they were not good enough to go into a blend!

▼ **After a tasting it's possible to buy a bottle of cask-strength whisky.** (Cath Harries)

Some whiskies to look out for

Brora

Located in the north-east of Scotland opposite Clynelish distillery, Brora has a cult following. It is regarded as one of the most interesting distilleries in Scotland, yet very little is known about it. This distillery was originally called Clynelish, but in around 1967 a new distillery with the same name was built across the road. According to the Whisky Exchange, casks from both distilleries were marked as Clynelish for a year or so until the Scotch Whisky Association asked for the name of one of these distilleries to be changed. The old distillery was then renamed Brora and finally closed in 1983.

Port Ellen

The prices of Port Ellen releases have shot up in recent years – for example, from £125 in 2007 to £185 in 2008 – and they are

continuing to rise, probably reflecting the diminution of Diageo's stock.

The Macallan Fine & Rare Collection

Among The Macallan's oldest maturing stock, the Fine & Rare Collection is a splendid range of vintage single-malts. Each year the range is expanded by the introduction of a new vintage release, with the earliest bottle having been distilled in 1926; most of the post-war years are represented in the collection.

(Cath Harries)

Turning whisky into gold

The early alchemists, experimenting with distillation, failed to turn their concoctions into gold. However, there are some who believe there is gold to be made from buying and selling rare whiskies.

The sums of money fetched by rare whiskies can be staggering. Early in 2014 a world record was set for the most expensive single-malt whisky sold at auction when a unique crystal decanter filled with rare Macallan M whisky fetched £380,000 at a Sotheby's auction in Hong Kong.

Why so much? First, the bottle is special. The faceted crystal decanter of the Macallan Imperiale M is called the Constantine – after the Roman emperor – and it holds six litres of whisky. One of only four bottles of its kind, this

◄ **How much do you like whisky? Would you pay £380,000 for this?** (Macallan)

▼ **Many collectors would be attracted to buy this because of the design of the decanter...** (Macallan)

▲ **Elaborate and unique bottle designs often attract investors.** (Cath Harries)

▲ **Bowmore's special releases are much sought after by collectors.** (Cath Harries)

▲ **Rarity and quality only add to the value of an expression.** (Cath Harries)

Constantine took 17 craftsmen over 50 hours to complete and 40 attempts were required before the perfect item was finally produced.

And then, of course, the bottle's contents are special. To create the perfect blend for M, Macallan's whisky blender spent two years choosing seven casks out of nearly 200,000. The age of the selected casks ranged from 25 to 75 years.

In 2012 Bowmore sold the No. 1 bottle of its oldest ever expression – the exceptionally rare Bowmore 1957, 54 Years Old – for £100,000. The money raised was all donated to Scottish charities. The bottle – one of only 12 in existence – is not only the oldest whisky the distillery has ever released, but also the oldest Islay single-malt ever released. This whisky is said to have flavours of blueberries and wild figs with mellow almond, tropical fruit and rich oak overtones. And if that is not enough, there are notes of dark chocolate and grapefruit, finishing with a hint of cassis, bergamot and star anise.

Another collectible is The Rolling Stones 50th Anniversary Whisky, of which only 150 bottles were produced. Crafted by

▶ **The value of a Rolling Stones 50th anniversary whisky could really rock one day!** (Beam Suntory)

Japanese distillers Suntory, this special blend contains malts distilled and casked in milestone years throughout the band's career, including 1962 (the band's formation), 1971 (the year the lips and tongue logo was unveiled) and 1990 (the first appearance in Japan's Tokyo Dome).

Even more rare – and probably undrinkable – are two bottles of whisky salvaged from the shipwreck that inspired the book and film *Whisky Galore*. Recently sold at auction for more than £10,000, these collectors' items were part of the cargo of the 8,000-tonne SS *Politician*, which sank off the shores of Eriskay, in the Outer Hebrides, in 1941. However, be warned, for another bottle from the same batch dropped from its 1997 value of £1,400 (when sold at auction by Christie's) to £1,300 seven years later; its original seal had been replaced and it was noted that the level of the liquid in the bottle had begun to decrease!

So can an ordinary person go about making money from collecting whisky? The answer is 'yes': the right bottle or collection of Scottish single-malt whisky is increasingly viewed as a viable alternative investment of choice. But like all markets in such assets – whether art, antiques, classic cars or fine wine – let the buyer beware that what goes up can go down.

Collector Mahesh Patel, who hosts an annual trade show in Las Vegas called the Universal Whisky Experience, advises would-be investors always to go for limited-edition bottles.

'Whisky prices follow the simple logic of supply and demand,' says Patel. 'Don't go for something off the shelf, even if it's 10, 12 or even 80 years old, because those are generally not limited production. Those are created every year, whereas limited-run productions are maybe 100 bottles or 10,000 bottles. At 10,000 bottles, they're going to be lower in price, but as people drink them, supply gets reduced and the prices go up.'

Bottles from certain distilleries are far more sought-after than others. As well as producing good whisky, distilleries that actively cater for the collectors' and investors' market include Macallan, Dalmore, Ardbeg, Lagavulin, Glenfiddich and Highland Park. As a general rule, whiskies that tend to attract most investor attention are those only available in very limited quantities that have been aged in the cask for between 10 and 60 years before being bottled.

▼ **Many collectors make a point of only investing in whiskies from one distillery, such as Glenfiddich.** (Cath Harries)

£1,250.00
Glenfiddich 1968 30yo
49.6% 70cl

£2,999.00
Glenfiddich 40yo / 45.4% /
70cl / Bot 2008 / OB

£15,000.00
Glenfiddich 50yo 46.1%
70cl

£599.00
The Dalmore 25yo / 42% /
70cl / OB

THE WORLD OF WHISKY

▲ Whiskies from closed distilleries such as Brora are much
sought after by collectors. (Cath Harries)

Glasgow auction website Scotch Whisky Auctions says that
whiskies at its auctions include jaw-droppingly rare bottles,
both very old and very new, mixed with hard-to-finds, easy-to-
buys and everything in between.

Bottles with investment potential need not cost the earth.
One good example of a successful 'investment grade' Scotch
released in 2011 was the Macallan Royal Marriage, which is
a combination of two casks, one from 29 April 1996 and the
other from 29 April 1999. The cost of a bottle new was £150
but within three years a bottle was sold at auction for £1,300.

Whisky from certain closed distilleries – known as
lost distilleries – are performing exceptionally well as an
investment. Two of the most popular are Port Ellen and
Brora. Both distilleries closed in 1983 so no more whisky was
produced from that date, but stocks still exist in casks.

Only time will tell if Diageo's release in 2012 of 160
bottles of Brora 40-Year-Old, the most expensive single-malt
whisky the company has ever released, will be a worthwhile
investment. Drawn from a single cask distilled in 1972 at a
cask strength of 59.1%, this whisky – the first 40-year-old
Brora whisky ever to be bottled – was priced at £6,995 a
bottle. To complete the package, the decanter is presented
in a beautiful wooden case designed as an interpretation of
the closed Brora distillery, skilfully handcrafted by the Queen's
cabinetmakers, N.E.J. Stevenson.

Top ten tips for investment

- Go for limited editions – fewer of them are around,
  with some limited editions released in tens of
  bottles rather than thousands.
- Buy upon retail release – this can be the route to
  higher gains.
- Go for independents – likely to be more sought-
  after.
- Pick the
  right bottle
  – look
  out for
  innovative
  bottle and
  packaging
  design.
- Choose lost
  distilleries –
  the bottlings
  are always
  rare.
- Go for old
  measures –
  fluid ounces
  rather than
  centilitres.
- Do not buy
  cases of
  standard bottles – unless you plan to drink the
  whisky yourself.
- Do not panic – make sure you do your whisky
  homework and know your drams.
- Be wary of scams – if something looks too good to
  be true, it probably is; always seek advice.
- Do your research – use social media and the web
  to find out about new releases.

(Cath Harries)

Was this entrancing site chosen to make whisky because it is far from the beady eyes of excise officers? (Cath Harries)

Islay of drams

Is Islay (pronounced *eye-ler*) the most famous whisky island in the world? It seems remarkable that one of Scotland's Western Isles, only 25 miles by 20, can be home to so many world-renowned distilleries – and there are plans for more to open. For any fan of whisky, Islay is certainly an island of dreams – and drams.

The distilleries in the south of Islay – Lagavulin, Ardbeg and Laphroaig – create the most strongly smoky, medicinal-flavoured, phenolic whiskies anywhere in the world, while those to the north – Bunnahabhain, Bowmore, Caol Ila and Bruichladdich – tend to have a lighter character. A newcomer, Kilchoman, is showing that it is still possible to make a whisky using organic barley exclusively grown on the island. And to these soon will be added the Port Charlotte and Gartbreck distilleries – two that are under construction as this book is written.

Most of Islay's distilleries use a high proportion of peat, dug and dried on the island, when malting the barley used for production. Bowmore, Kilchoman and Laphroaig still have their own floor maltings.

Once there were many more distilleries on the island and some, like Port Ellen (now a maltings) are among Scotland's famed lost distilleries – meaning that their whiskies are still available but in ever-dwindling volumes and at ever-increasing prices.

It is believed that Irish monks introduced the art of distillation to Islay during the early 14th century. Ireland is only 25 miles (40km) away, although that still must have been quite a journey in a coracle.

The island is perfect for whisky production not just because of its remoteness (which in the past meant that it was far from interfering customs officers) but also for its abundance of peat for fuel, good water and fertile hinterland where barley was grown. Its climate also favours the maturation of whisky.

ARDBEG

Ardbeg is the last of three distilleries on the road that leads eastwards along the south coast of Islay from Port Ellen. Collectively known as the Kildalton distilleries, the trio also includes Lagavulin and Laphroaig.

The distillery was founded in 1815 by John Macdonald, but there is no doubt that distilling started much earlier, with smugglers attracted to its coastal location, peaty water from the Loch Uigeadail and abundance of peat. Like many distilleries, it has seen its ups and downs: in the 1980s it was mothballed and it was nearly demolished in 1996, but in 1997 Glenmorangie took control and its fortunes have risen to new heights. Sadly, the floor maltings and kilns were closed but today they have been transformed into a smart shop and café.

A highlight of a tour is the stunning view over the sea from the pristine room that houses six washbacks made of Oregon pine. Ardbeg's shapely pair of stills, proportioned like lamp glasses, are also notable; they have an extra purifier, which comes off the lyne arm and contributes to the spirit's unique flavours.

▲ Open windows allow sea breezes to caress Ardberg's wash. (Cath Harries)

▼ Whisky's renaissance has seen much-needed investment in distilleries which once faced demolition. (Cath Harries)

▲ A good selection of grain is at the heart of the finest whiskies. (Cath Harries)

▼ The fermentation of the mash is a crucial part of whisky's journey from the distillery to the glass. (Cath Harries)

▲ It is said the shape of a still has a profound effect on the quality of the spirit it produces. (Cath Harries)

▼ Most whisky distillers keep a large stock of bourbon barrels ready for future use. (Cath Harries)

Can there be a more picturesque distillery than Bowmore? (Cath Harries)

▶ The gates might be large, but the welcome is even bigger at the Bowmore distillery. (Cath Harries)

BOWMORE

Bowmore is the oldest distillery on Islay. It was founded in 1779 by farmer David Simpson at its coastal location on Loch Indaal and it dominates the town, the island's largest, that has grown up there.

The peaty water for its two pairs of wash and spirit stills comes from the nearby River Laggan. The smell of peat permeates the building from the furnace that dries the germinated malt created in the distillery's own floor maltings. There is a smart-looking mash tun and six Oregon pine washbacks stand in a line, each named after a previous owner of the distillery. Heat created from the distillation is put to good use as it warms the water in the adjacent swimming pool.

The Bowmore distillery is famed for the age of its whiskies. The oldest barrel on site was filled in 1967, but the oldest one in store on the mainland hails from 1957.

Much of the complexity of Bowmore's whiskies comes from storage in sherry casks, although port or Bordeaux barrels have been used too. The distillery manager says that one of the best ways to appreciate the contents of a cask is to take a sample using a valinch (a large pipette), rub the spirit on your hands and inhale deeply the sensuous, swirling aromas.

▼ Each of Bowmore's washbacks is named after a previous owner of the distillery. (Cath Harries)

▲ Two pairs of stills operate side by side to produce some of the world's greatest whisky. (Cath Harries)

◀ It doesn't matter how advanced the technology is, someone has to decide where the spirit flows. (Cath Harries)

▼ More than 27,000 casks are stored in Bowmore's dunnages. (Cath Harries)

THE WORLD OF WHISKY 2

BRUICHLADDICH

Bruichladdich distillery (pronounced *brook-laddie*) was founded in 1881 and remains very little changed despite a rebuild in 1886 and an extension in 1975.

Inside it is a perfect example of Victorian engineering genius, with each stage of production easily and almost seamlessly moving from one stage of production to the next in an elegant square dance around the distillery's yard.

Much of the equipment is original and has been carefully restored, including the original open seven-ton mash tun. The beating heart of the distillery has to be its still room, which spreads over two floors and is dominated by its extremely tall and narrow-necked stills. Here, they say, distilling follows an oral tradition and nothing is written down, let alone entered into a computer. Here distilling is an art and craft. The distillery also produces its own gin on the venerable Ugly Betty still.

A highlight of any visit has to be a tour of the distillery's warehouse, where the whisky matures for long years and the angels' share fills the air with sweet smells of orange and Christmas pudding flavours. Some visitors are lucky enough to have tastings straight from the barrel.

In July 2012 the distillery was purchased by Rémy Cointreau, which says it does not want to change anything – an admirable philosophy.

▼**Much of the equipment might be old but progress is measured in drams at Bruichladdich.** (Cath Harries)

▲ **A silent still stands proud outside the Bruichladdich distillery.** (Cath Harries)

▶**A traditional chalk board beats a computer at Bruichladdich.** (Cath Harries)

▼ **The Lomond still, possibly the oldest in the world, is used to make gin.** (Cath Harries)

WHISKY MANUAL 73

▲ At the end of a long, narrow, twisting, steep lane stands Bunnahabhain.
(Cath Harries)

▼ If stills could talk, this wizened trio would tell the story of the light spirit they produce. (Cath Harries)

BUNNAHABHAIN

At the Bunnahabhain distillery (pronounced *booner-harb-en*) they say that the stills tell stories. Large and onion-shaped, they are – unlike most other stills – unpolished and unoiled, which gives them an enigmatic, mysterious, wizened character. If only they could talk.

Founded in 1881 by William and James Greenless, Bunnahabhain is probably the most isolated of the island's distilleries, but that does not stop many whisky fans walking to it from Port Askaig and enjoying fantastic views of the Paps of Jura and the wildness of the surrounding hills.

A ship's bell marked Diana hangs near the entrance – testament to the dangerous waters of the nearby wild Atlantic as three ships of the same name have all foundered in the bay.

The distillery's building can seem grey and sombre but there is a light vivacity to its whiskies. The floral nature of the whisky doubtless comes from the soft peaty water drawn from a stream fed by Loch Staoinsha.

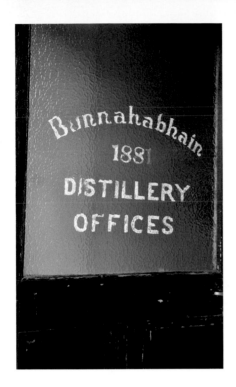

▲ It wasn't until the 1990s that Bunnahabhain produced its first peated whisky. (Cath Harries)

▲ Most distilleries polish their stills, but not at Bunnahabhain, where nature takes its course. (Cath Harries)

▲ Once the bells tolled for a sinking ship, now they ring for the success of a vibrant distillery. (Cath Harries)

▼ A mix of sherry and bourbon casks help to create Bunnahabhain's eclectic drams. (Cath Harries)

CAOL ILA

From the modern, glass-fronted still house at the Caol Ila distillery (pronounced *cull-eela*) there are great views over the Sound of Islay, from which comes the distillery's Gaelic name. And the road to the distillery, which has a wild, picturesque setting, is still as steep as when whisky chronicler Alfred Barnard visited and preferred to walk the final section rather than stay in his dog cart, much to the irritation of his driver.

Hector Henderson, a Glasgow businessman with a keen interest in distilling, built the original distillery in 1846. In his day Barnard described the distillery as modern, and indeed it still is today. It was recently closed for a couple of years for rebuilding and installation of state-of-the-art distilling equipment.

Now part of Diageo, Caol Ila is best known for whiskies that lack the iodine intensity of flavours that some of the other distillers on the island produce.

▶ **This 20-year-old Caol Ila whisky was bottled in 1996 to celebrate the distillery's 150th anniversary.**
(Cath Harries)

KILCHOMAN

Kilchoman, which opened in 2005, is the first new distillery on Islay for 124 years. Remote and only accessible down a track to Rockside Farm, it is a modern throwback to an era in which many farms would have had their own distillery. But back then many stills would have been illegal – Kilchoman is strictly legal!

The distillery has its own small floor maltings and peat-fired kiln to produce its smoky whiskies and Rockside Farm also grows some of the barley it uses. Its first expressions have now been released and include a Kilchoman 100% Islay, made only with barley from the farm and malted on site.

▲ **Kilchoman's distinctive whiskies are bottled and labelled by hand.** (Cath Harries)

▼ **A working farm is home to one of Islay's newest distilleries.**
(Cath Harries)

◀ Islay's first new distillery for more than 120 years has its own flood distillery.
(Cath Harries)

▲ A smart shop is an essential part of Kilchoman's visitor centre. (Cath Harries)

LAGAVULIN

Lagavulin was founded by John Johnston in 1816 and is now owned by Diageo. Its smoked malt comes from the Port Ellen maltings and this, together with peated water from the Solan Lochs in the hills above the distillery, helps produce its distinctive drams, which have their own briny intensity.

Alfred Barnard judged that 'there could have been no prettier or more romantic spot chosen for a distillery'. The Lagavulin site is said to be one of the oldest distilling locations on Islay and it is thought that the first distillery was built in 1742. Prior to that, stated Barnard, it 'consisted of ten small and separate bothys for the manufacture of moonlight'. Barnard said the term 'moonlight' was used to describe illicit whisky, 'in contradistinction to that which paid duty, which was termed daylight'.

▶ Lagavulin's location is regarded as one of the most perfect spots for distilling. (Cath Harries)

▲ Islay's abundant peat plays a major part in the flavour of Laphroaig's whiskies. (Cath Harries)

▲ Sea breezes are said to contribute to Laphroaig's 'reek' character. (Laphroaig)

LAPHROAIG

Alfred Barnard described the whisky made at Laphroaig as being much sought-after by blenders because of its exceptional quality and its 'peculiar peat reek flavour'. And contrary to what many of today's Islay distillers say, Barnard asserted that the coastal location of most of the island's distilleries 'has no effect whatever on the whisky'. The 'thick and pungent' flavours, stated Barnard, came from the island's abundant peat, which is heavily flavoured with sphagnum moss.

The fact that peat is important at Laphroaig (pronounced *la-froyg*) is evidenced inside the visitor centre by a display

▼ The depth and quality of Laphroaig's peat bog can clearly be seen. (Cath Harries)

▼ Friends of Laphroaig have their own boots for walking in the peat bogs. (Cath Harries)

▼ The distillery's kiln is heated by peat heavy with sphagnum moss. (Cath Harries)

▶ **The smoke from the kiln rises up through the drying malt and imparts its smoky flavours.** (Cath Harries)

▶ ▶ **The germinating malt requires frequent turning – back-breaking work, which is done by hand.**
(Cath Harries)

of smart but used wellington boots belonging to Friends of Laphroaig, a fan club for lovers of the whisky that Prince Charles proclaimed to be 'the finest in the world'. Launched in 1994, the Friends of Laphroaig is quite a community and every one of the half a million or so of them receives a lifetime lease on a square foot of an Islay peat bog. Over the years there have been some extraordinary sights at Laphroaig, including a wedding between two Friends, the scattering of a Friend's ashes and the installation of a Japanese ceremonial garden.

The distillery still has its own malting floor and a kiln which is fired by island-dried peat and breezes off the sea.

The large characterful glass-fronted still house at Laphroaig stands across a courtyard from maltings. Inside there are three wash stills and four spirit stills. On a summer's day the heat can seem overbearing, but it clearly is a good place to work on the long nights of winter.

Founded by brothers Alexander and Donald Johnston in 1815, the distillery was one of the first in Scotland to use bourbon barrels for maturation.

On Islay there certainly is a community of spirit which sustains not only the island's once again growing population but the interests of whisky fans worldwide.

▶ **The shape and size of each still it is said to give different flavours to the final spirit.**
(Cath Harries)

The Islay distilleries

Ardbeg
Port Ellen PA42 7EA
www.ardbeg.com

Bowmore
School Street, Bowmore PA43 7GS
www.bowmore.co.uk

Bruichladdich
Bruichladdich PA49 7UN
www.bruichladdich.com

Bunnahabhain
Shore Street, Port Askaig PA46 7RP
www.bunnahabhain.com

Caol Ila
Port Askaig PA46 7RL
www.malts.com

Kilchoman
Rockside Farm, Bruichladdich PA49 7UT
www.kilchomandistillery.com

Lagavulin
Port Ellen PA42 7DZ
www.malts.com

Laphroaig
Port Ellen PA42 7DU
www.laphroaig.com

Some Scottish shorts

In this section we take a look at five far-flung distilleries of varied character that provide an interesting cross-section of whisky distilling in Scotland: Ben Nevis, Clynelish, Jura, Oban and Tobermory.

BEN NEVIS

The Ben Nevis distillery is one of the oldest licensed distilleries in Scotland and is located literally in the shadow of Scotland's highest mountain, after which it is named. It is from this mountain that water flows for the distillery's whisky making.

'Long John' McDonald, a 6ft 4in descendant of a ruler of the western Scottish kingdom of Argyll, established the distillery in 1825. Queen Victoria visited it in 1848 with her six-year-old son, the Prince of Wales (later to become Edward VII), who was given a cask of whisky, which was moved duty-free to Buckingham Palace. In 1886 the whisky chronicler Alfred Barnard described the towering mountain as 'gloomy' but he also stated that the distillery was thriving.

In 1941 the McDonald family sold the distillery to Canadian millionaire Joseph Hobbs and in 1955 it became one of the few

in Scotland to have both pot stills and a Coffey continuous still, a situation that continued for many years. It was sold to Whitbread in 1981 and closed in 1986. Japanese whisky-makers Nikka acquired the distillery in 1989 and woke it from its enforced slumber. Today it produces a range of quality single-malt and blended-malt whiskies under the name Dew of Ben Nevis, while one of its new-make spirits is sent to Japan for blending into Nikka black whisky.

Today, sadly, there is something faded and down at heel about this clearly once-proud, vibrant distillery, for much of its fabric looks in urgent need of refurbishment, not helped by the black Baudoinia fungus that stains many walls; this fungus lives on ethanol and therefore thrives on the 'angels' share' whisky found in distilleries and whisky warehouses.

▼ ◥ **One of Scotland's oldest distilleries is in the shadow of often mist-covered Ben Nevis.** (Cath Harries)

CLYNELISH

For anyone driving north from Inverness to John O'Groats, perhaps heading onwards to Orkney to sample the delights of its whisky, the Clynelish distillery and its visitor centre at the popular coastal holiday town of Brora, Sutherland, is the perfect place to take a break, an hour up the A9 from Inverness, about halfway along the route. As with most distilleries, the location – on the north side of the plain that forms the Strath Bora – is beautiful and remote.

Clynelish distillery was founded in 1819 by the Duke of Sutherland, but since then it has had many owners and suffered many of the trials and tribulations of the whisky industry – including bankruptcy, change of ownership and the mothballing of the site. The current distillery was opened in 1967, next to the site of the original Brora distillery.

Now part of Diageo, the international drinks giant that

▲ **Distillers bring much needed investment and jobs to remote Scottish communities.** (Diageo)

owns 12 distilleries in Scotland, Clynelish is the company's most northerly distiller and has received significant investment. In recent times an additional mash tun, ten more washbacks and six more copper stills have been installed. The result is that production of the distillery's famously waxy single-malt spirit has increased to over 10 million litres a year. It is unique in both taste and texture, and highly prized by Diageo's master blenders for use in world-leading brands such as Johnnie Walker.

Clynelish is also a single-malt whisky in its own right and its expressions include a cask-strength whisky that is fresh-tasting, exuding grapes and melon flavours with vanilla notes from the American oak bourbon casks.

JURA

On the island of Jura they say that today's rain is tomorrow's whisky. And rain is indeed vital for the Isle of Jura distillery's whisky production. Water to feed the distillery's Bhaille Mharghaidh spring comes only from the sky and a dry summer, therefore, can see production suspended until the spring is replenished.

The distillery stands in the centre of Jura's only village, Craighouse. On a warm summer's day it's an idyllic spot, where palm trees grow, and there are fine views of Small Isles Bay and its islands as well as the more distant Scottish mainland. Visitors can get here by first taking the ferry to Islay and then another small, clanking ferry over the sometimes tempestuous Sound of Islay.

Distilling has taken place here for hundreds of years, both illegally and legally, and the spirit made must have warmed many a heart over the island's long, dark winter months.

The still room rises like a church's nave and its congregation of four tall, graceful stills are some of the tallest in Scotland. Two were installed in 1963 when the distillery was brought back from the dead after two of the island's landowners, Robin Fletcher and Tony Riley-Smith, decided that one way to improve the island's stuttering economy would be to rebuild the distillery, which was in a sad state of disrepair, having long since lost its roof, which was removed to avoid tax having to be paid on the building. In 1978 capacity was doubled when two more stills were installed and great care was taken to match them to the existing stills in order to ensure that the character of the spirit did not change.

In 1994 the Jura Distillery Company Ltd was taken over by Whyte & Mackay. Today its complex malts – light, delicate and floral in character but tinged with a briny note – are thriving.

▼ **On a summer's day Jura is idyllic – spending a winter on the island is said to require true grit.** (Cath Harries)

▲ Distilleries have a scrupulous inventory of each and every barrel of spirit. (Cath Harries)

◀ Jura's graceful stills are four of the tallest in Scotland. (Cath Harries)

▲ After a period of closure, production at Jura was doubled in 1978. (Cath Harries)

▼ Whisky production on Jura was probably illegal for many years, but now it is all strictly above board. (Cath Harries)

OBAN

One of Scotland's smallest distilleries is located in the engaging coastal town of Oban, where bustling ferries frequently come and go, taking travellers out to the distant islands.

Brothers John and Hugh Stevenson established Oban distillery in 1794 on the site of a former brewery. It still occupies its original buildings, which are dominated by a towering red-banded, black-topped chimney. Few other distilleries in Scotland have such a vibrant location, with the busy town on three sides and sheer rock behind.

Popular with visitors, it has a thriving shop and a fine display telling the story of the distillery. But this is no static whisky museum, as it remains a working distillery. Its wash tun and washbacks are lit so that visitors can get a clear view of their interiors. And the experienced guides clearly delight in explaining the finer points of distilling and whisky making.

◄ **Oban distillery's distinctive chimney dominates the lower part of this important port.** (Cath Harries)

▼ **The Oban distillery is unusual in that it is based at the heart of a busy town.** (Cath Harries)

▲ Oban's stills produce a light and zesty spirit – and some say even a taste of the sea. (Cath Harries)

The shape of the two hard-working stills, with their worms placed high at the top, is said to be the reason why the distillery produces whisky with light, zesty, orange flavours and a touch of brininess. A special treat for visitors on a distillery tour is that they get offered a taste of the whisky, straight from the barrel in the former cooperage.

Small it might be, but Oban has a big reputation and its single-malt whisky is part of Diageo's Classic Malts Collection.

◄ A highlight of any distillery tour has to be a taste of whisky drawn straight from a barrel. (Cath Harries)

▼ Nothing goes to waste – spent grains are made into a nutritious animal feed. (Cath Harries)

▲ ◥ Tourism and whisky are vital to the economy on Mull.
(Cath Harries)

'Scottish shorts' distilleries

Ben Nevis

Lochy Bridge, Fort William PH33 6TJ
www.bennevisdistillery.com

Clynelish

Brora, Sutherland KW9 6LR
www.discovering-distilleries.com/clynelish

Jura

Craighouse, Isle of Jura PA60 7XT
www.isleofjura.com

Oban

Oban, Argyll PA34 5NH
www.malts.com

Tobermory

Isle of Mull, Argyll PA75 6NR
www.tobermorymalt.com

TOBERMORY

Tobermory is located in the picturesque fishing village of the same name on Mull, the third-largest of the Hebridean isles and the easiest to reach from the mainland by ferry from Oban. Originally called Ledaig, the distillery was built by John Sinclair and dates back to 1798. It is small but perfectly formed, comprising a courtyard at the harbourside.

Over the years the distillery has passed through many hands and had long periods of use for other purposes, such as power generation and the storage of cheese. Many thought it was the end of the road for the distillery in 1975 when the Ledaig distillery company filed for bankruptcy, but in 1979 a property company bought the premises and the Tobermory Distillery Company was born. Production stopped again in 1985 followed by another restart in 1989. The distillery was acquired by Burn Stewart in 1993 and became part of the Distell group in 2013.

Today the distillery's four tall, shapely pot stills are hard at work producing peaty and non-peaty whiskies. The distillery is best known for its ten-year-old Tobermory single-malt, produced using unpeated Scottish malt. The original Ledaig name is not lost, as it is used for a peated Scotch made with malt from the Port Ellen maltings on Islay.

Today, very few barrels are kept on the site. Most of the output is instead sent to Burn Stewart's mainland distillery at Deanston, near Doune, for maturation.

THE LONDON DISTILLERY COMPANY

Instilling a new spirit in London

In 2013 the London Distillery Company was granted London's first licence to produce single-malt whisky in more than a century, since the Lea Valley distillery in Stratford closed in 1903. A tiny producer with big ambitions, it is restoring the spirit of pride to the UK's capital.

There is a funky feel to the London Distillery, which is based in an old dairy and ice store in Battersea, south of the river. Overlooking Ransome's Dock, it shares its urban-chic space with theatre designers, artists, Barry McGuigan's boxing gym and a well-used table-tennis table – a favourite with local web and app designers.

The new London Distillery's co-founder, Darren Rook, is on a mission to educate people about whisky and its ingredients. He is one of a growing band of new producers who are daring to be different by making whiskies that reflect the heritage and culture of their area by adopting local customs, grains and production methods to produce a whisky that is unique.

Rook is keen to talk about the yeasts and malts he uses in the spirit his company makes. Indeed he sounds more like a brewer than the chief executive of a distillery as he enthuses about the attributes of different yeast strains and varieties of malt.

'It has taken just over three years of hard work from the early concept to get to where we are today,' explains Rook.

▲ **The London Distillery is at the beginning of a long journey to make its own whisky.** (Cath Harries)

▼ **Darren Rook oversees spirit production in his shiny new distillery.** (Cath Harries)

'This is really only the start of the journey as we have some time until the whisky reaches its optimum condition. We're aiming to create an historical style of single-malt with a great depth of flavour and floral backbone. That said, thanks to our small size and our equipment, we are not limited to one style. One fermentation will fill one cask, so we are able to experiment and create bespoke whiskies.'

Each boutique batch is different and Rook is experimenting with different temperatures and times for the mash and fermentation. Currently he uses different yeasts for each wash and he has used strains from at least two former London brewers, Whitbread and Young's. His barley malt comes from a small batch producer of malt, Warminster Maltings in Wiltshire, who still use traditional floor maltings where much of the work is done by hand. For one wash he used organic lager malt, but he has also used older-style barley malts such as Plumage Archer, Golden Promise and Maris Otter, varieties that were much favoured by English ale brewers and whisky makers.

As part of his aspiration to make each barrel batch of spirit unique, Rook plans to marry barley varieties with yeast strains of different eras to see if they make a 'dram' of difference to the final spirit – 'all part of our desire to educate people'.

Next to his two fermentation tanks stand blue plastic barrels filled with the fruits of his first distillations. It is with infectious enthusiasm that he takes the top off each barrel to ingest their aromas – each is pronounced and each is different. One is bready, another has swathes of orange zest; one smells like fresh blackberry pie and another has waves of tomato relish.

For someone who is only 31, Rook is almost wishing his life away as he imagines what the finished whiskies will be like when, after three years, he can broach the first bottles. Indeed, he is already looking forward to his young children's 18th and 21st birthdays, when their health will be toasted with spirits he is making now. Making whisky is certainly a long-term project.

Currently there is only enough equipment to produce about 100 casks a year – two per week. Each fermentation takes five days and produces about 2,000 litres of wash. This is split into two batches: the first distillation produces around 650–700 litres and the second distillation results in enough spirit to fill one cask.

Rook is also clearly going to have as much fun selecting individual wooden barrels as he has had choosing his grain and yeast. On my visit two brand-new English oak barrels, full of water, lay next to the lauter tun in which the grain is cooked; filling them with water allows the wood to rehydrate and breathe. Lightly charred on the inside, these barrels had been made by one of England's last coopers, Alastair Simms, who worked at Wadworth Brewery in Devizes, Wiltshire. Rook also has plans to use former bourbon barrels of American oak and chestnut, the latter a wood once favoured for storing wine and spirits. Barrels that once stored port and sherry will undoubtedly find their way into his ambitious repertoire.

▲ **Darren Rook named his whisky still after his Scottish grandmother.** (Cath Harries)

At the London distillery the whisky is distilled in a beautiful 650-litre copper pot still, Matilda, named after Rook's Scottish grandmother, and a four-plate distillation column, which produces drier, subtler flavours. Rook has so much confidence in his business that a second, even bigger 750-litre copper pot still, Hilda, was on the way when I visited – not bad for a company that had yet to see its first whisky go on sale.

▼ **Tours of the London Distillery are likely to become very popular.** (Cath Harries)

Cry St George for England – and now whisky

This is the story of St George's Distillery at Roudham, Norfolk. You can smell the angels' share as you step inside one of the three warehouses, where the air is heavy with the sweet flavours of Jim Beam bourbon and Pedro Ximénez sherry. If an atmosphere could be intoxicating, then this is certainly it.

Distiller David Fitt is proud of his barrels, especially the one signed by Prince Charles when he visited the English Whisky Co at St George's Distillery on 27 March 2007. Like a shepherd tending his flock, Fitt knows where every barrel is, and which batch of spirit each one contains, and how long it has been maturing.

▲ **St George's Distillery has a smart visitor centre and shop that sells more than 200 single-malts and cask-strength malts from around the world.** (Cath Harries)

▶ **St George's distiller David Fitt loves to talk about his creations.** (Cath Harries)

▲ As the whisky matures, the barrels are regularly moved to a different location in the dunnage. (Cath Harries)

▼ As whisky matures some of it will be lost due to evaporation through the wood of the barrel – this is known as the angels' share. A glass-fronted barrel at St George's enables the loss to be clearly seen. David's finger marks the spot where the cask was filled to on 14 October 2010. Almost four years later the lower level of the spirit can be clearly viewed. In this small barrel David estimates that 4% of the volume is lost each year. In Scotland, with its cooler climate, a loss of only 1% is expected. Whisky maturing in the heat of India could lose 12% a year. (Cath Harries)

Each barrel is carefully looked after and from time to time moved to another location in the bonded warehouse, so that it is subject to slightly different temperatures and humidity. This process rouses the slowly maturing spirit, encouraging new flavours and developing the diversity of each cask's character. Periodically the bung from each barrel will be removed and the contents thoughtfully nosed to assess its characteristics – floral, fruity or spicy, or a combination?

It is primarily wood that gives whisky its thousands of flavour compounds and each batch of spirit will spend time in barrels that contained either bourbon, port or sherry. Each of these previous inhabitants of a cask brings different shades and nuances to the final whisky.

St George's Distillery creates both unpeated and peated whiskies, as well as having a rolling programme of cask trials. Some St George's whisky is bottled from a single cask, others from a blend of casks (often four of them), and the contents of each barrel will provide the chorus of notes with which Fitt will create his spiritual symphonies. He likes his whisky to be tonal and balanced: if whisky distillers can be compared with composers of music, Fitt is more Wolfgang Amadeus Mozart than John Cage.

The distillery is owned by the Nelstrops, a family deeply involved in farming. At the start of the new millennium James Nelstrop and his son Andrew decided to investigate a subject close to James's heart – whisky production. The best barley is grown in Norfolk, some of it by the Nelstrops, and the Breckland water is superb, requiring only filtration before it can be used in the distillery. Several design concepts were considered, a great deal of research was done in Scotland, Ireland and Wales, and planning approval was finally granted in January 2006, more than 100 years since whisky production had ceased in England. Although the initial idea was for a micro-distillery, HM Revenue and Customs would not permit the stills to be smaller than 1,800 litres – larger than some in Scotland.

In December 2006 the first 29 barrels of English whisky were made and by August 2007 St George's Distillery opened to the public with a visitor centre, whisky shop and tours. Since the original distillations, more than 2,000 casks have been made. The water for St George's comes from the distillery's own well, the cap of which can be seen at the front of the distillery on its smart lawn, which leads to a pleasant riverside walk.

The first stage of whisky making at St George's is to mash the grain in the distillery's smart mash tun. Once the warm water and crushed malted grain have been mixed, a process that takes about seven hours, the porridge-like liquid is left to stand for an hour – a trick commonly used by brewers to draw all the fermentable goodness out of the grain. According to Fitt, some distillers rush this process.

The liquid is drained and then sparging – a term that means running hot water through the grain – is done three times, a process that draws even more of the much-needed fermentable sugars from the malt.

▶ The fermented wash, which is a crude form of ale, as it is a beer made without hops, is not much to look at. Cloudy and yellow, it is about 8% ABV; most of the fermentable sugars will have been turned into alcohol. (Cath Harries)

The liquid is then transferred into one of the distillery's two fermentation vessels where the yeast is added to start the fermentation process. The resulting wort, which is collected at around 16.5°C, moves to the first of the distillery's two shapely-looking pot stills where it is distilled to about 23% ABV. The spirit now has a second distillation, with the resultant new-make spirit being 73% ABV. Fitt likes to run the spirit into the spirit safe at around 17°C as he believes this creates a drink of the greatest complexity.

Clear to the eye, the new-make spirit will be diluted to about 63% ABV before being transferred into a wooden cask.

Like the chrysalis stage in a caterpillar's metamorphosis into a butterfly, the seemingly magical transformation of grain to whisky moves to its next stage, the final part of its journey to maturity and its final revealing as a true English whisky after many long months in different casks.

St George's Distillery can be found at Harling Road, Roudham, East Harling, Norfolk NR16 2QW. The website is www.englishwhisky.co.uk.

▼ For research purposes every expression bottled will have to be tasted. (Cath Harries)

Whisky from the Suffolk coast

Long known for its fine beers, Adnams of Southwold is now one of England's newest whisky distilleries. From grain to glass, its whisky is distilled from a wash made from East Anglian malted barley and wheat – plus oats from Scotland.

The malted barley, wheat and oats are milled, then mixed together with hot water in the Adnams Brewery's mash tun and heated to around 63°C. This releases the natural sugars in the barley to create the sugary liquid known as wort. Adnams' master brewer, Fergus Fitzgerald, then makes a beer wash that is fermented to around 6% ABV without the addition of hops. Throughout fermentation he carefully controls the temperature of the liquid so that he can regulate the metabolic

rate of the yeast to create unique flavours and aromas – just as he does for Adnams' beers.

The wash is then distilled in the beer-stripping column and moved into its copper pot stills. The stills heat the liquid, which evaporates at different levels in the column – with the 'hearts' becoming the new-make spirit. This high-strength, pure spirit, which has no colour at this stage, is then moved into new American oak casks and matured in Adnams' whisky dunnage and cellars in Southwold for more than three years. The American oak helps to create the whisky's bold coconut and chocolate flavours, and imparts a rich colour.

'Our Triple Grain Whisky is stylistically closer to American

▼ **An unused part of Adnams brewery has been transformed into a modern distillery.** (Cath Harries)

▶ The attractive coastal town of Southwold is dominated by Adnams.
(Cath Harries)

▼ The beer stripping column still, a copper pot still and Rectifying columns were all made in Germany.
(Cath Harries)

◢ The refurbished building now has a new lease of life as the Adnams Copper House Distillery.
(Cath Harries)

◀ **Adnams' distiller John McCarthy says oak gives whisky most of its colour and flavour.** (Cath Harries)

▲ **Jonathan Adnams loves to sample the aromas of his whiskies straight from the barrel.** (Cath Harries)

whiskeys than it is to its Scottish cousins,' states Adnams' distiller John McCarthy. 'This is in part due to its mix of malted grains – barley, wheat and oats – but mostly due to the use of toasted new American oak casks in its maturation. Scottish, Canadian and Irish whiskies tend to be matured in previously used oak casks – usually either ex-bourbon or sherry casks.

'The oak is extremely important as it imparts the majority of the flavours and colour. Triple Grain's bold and intense dark chocolate, toast, pepper, sweet honey and orange peel notes can be attributed to the interaction between our pure, high-strength spirit and our choice of new American oak barrels.'

Another Adnams whisky, its Single Malt No 1 at 43% ABV, has been matured exclusively in new French oak barrels and is also made from East Anglian barley; this is smooth and rich, with notes of runny honey, vanilla and apricot.

The company also makes an *eau de vie de bière* from its Broadside hopped beer. This is matured in heavily toasted Russian oak casks for 12 months and, unlike whisky, it can then be sold, while still quite young.

Adnams can be found at Sole Bay Brewery, Southwold, Suffolk IP18 6JW and the company's website is http://adnams.co.uk.

◀ **Adnams experiments with different grains and woods to produce its flavoursome whiskies.**
(Cath Harries)

Welsh whisky gold

There is gold in the Brecon Beacons. Some of it is for fools. But at the Penderyn Distillery in South Wales on the foothills of the glorious Brecon Beacons, with its sublime mix of sandstone and carboniferous rocks, there is liquid gold – and lots of it.

Whisky making is not new to Wales: in 1705 a distillery was founded in Dale, Pembrokeshire, by the Williams family, who later emigrated to the USA. There, in 1783, Evan Williams set up a distillery on the Ohio river at the foot of what is now Fifth Street in Louisville, thereby becoming Kentucky's first distiller on what is now known as Whiskey Row – perhaps it should be called Welsh Whiskey Row.

Back in Wales, the Welsh Distillery opened at Frongoch, near Bala, in 1890 but it did not last long, for it shut about ten years later – the temperance movement was not good for business and then the owner was run over by his own horse and cart. Another attempt to create a Welsh whisky, early in the 20th century, foundered after expensive litigation when a court judged that the company concerned could not be allowed to sell a whisky as Welsh when it was simply Scottish-made spirit bottled in Wales.

So when the Penderyn Distillery opened in 1999, therefore, it was the first new distillery in Wales for over 100 years. Its whiskies, unlike the nearby craggy slopes of the Brecons, are sumptuously smooth – and very much the real thing.

▲ **Penderyn was the first new distillery in Wales for more than 100 years.** (Cath Harries)

▼ **Wales and whisky have a history spanning more than 200 years.** (Cath Harries)

▲ **Business is good, as Penderyn is installing some new stills to keep up with demand.** (Cath Harries)

◥ **Prince Charles signed a cask of Penderyn whisky when the distillery first opened.** (Cath Harries)

▶ **Penderyn whiskies are matured in bourbon and Madeira barrels. An old bottle of Welsh whisky is on display in the visitor centre.** (Cath Harries)

Penderyn's single-malt whisky – *wysgi* in Welsh – was launched on 1 March 2004 and the company has gone from strength to strength since then.

The still at Penderyn is a unique variation of a tall Coffey still and a pot still, and was specially designed by Dr David Faraday, a descendent of the famous Victorian scientist Michael Faraday. The still is split into two so as to fit within the relatively low height of the building's rooftop, as required by planning regulations within the National Park.

Penderyn has experimented with the use of different woods and barrels to mature its light-bodied spirit, which ages and resonates in bourbon and Madeira barrels. For the initial maturation, the spirit is put into hand-selected bourbon barrels, and then it is transferred into Portuguese barrels, previously home to rich Madeira wine, where the *wysgi* undergoes its final, almost magical transformation. Each cask is closely watched and regularly nosed until the wood has given its full gift of flavour. It is an art, craft and science that can only be undertaken by trained whisky blenders – no machine could do it.

Business has been good at Penderyn, where there is a thriving visitor centre. Until recently the wash from which the whisky is distilled came from the Brains brewery in Cardiff, but now they make it themselves in a new mash tun. Two new pot stills have also been installed and no doubt they will make good use of them by creating and experimenting with new styles and expressions of single-malt Welsh whisky.

The distillery's address is Penderyn Distillery, Penderyn, Wales CF44 0SX and the company website is www.penderyn-distillery.co.uk.

Bushmills distillery has it all

Bushmills is rather special. The distillery is located in Northern Ireland in the pretty town of the same name, just two miles away from the Giant's Causeway, and distilling has taken place here for hundreds of years.

When, in 1608, King James I granted Sir Thomas Phillips a licence to distil, Bushmills became the world's first licensed distillery. According to Alfred Barnard's *The Whisky Distilleries of the United Kingdom*, it was in the hands of 'smugglers' in 1743, but by 1784 it was recognised once again as a legal distillery and by this time most of its 10,000 gallons of annual output was exported to the West Indies and North America. By the time of Barnard's visit almost a century later, production had increased to 100,000 gallons year, and then, as now, the USA was the biggest market.

As well as producing its softly spoken, unsmoked whiskeys, the Bushmills distillery is also a big visitor attraction nowadays, with over 100,000 people passing through each year – but no one is guaranteed to see Bushmills' resident ghost, the 'Grey Lady'. Many visitors also choose to travel along the magnificent coastal stretch of narrow-gauge railway from the historic town of Bushmills to the famous stone columns of the Giant's Causeway.

The distillery's source of water is Saint Columb's Rill, which is a tributary of the Bush river, from which the town takes its

▲ **Bushmills was the first licensed distillery in the world.** (Bushmills)

▼ **Close to the Giant's Causeway, Bushmills is a popular visitor attraction.** (Tim Hampson)

▲ **A good source of water is essential for whisky production.**
(Bushmills)

▲ **Bushmills casks once contained bourbon, Madeira or port.**
(Bushmills)

name; the Bush river is renowned for its salmon, which thrive in the crystal-clear water.

A tour of the Bushmills distillery starts by passing a cutaway display of an old mash tun in which the barley malt would have been mashed in times past, but today the shine of the old tun's copper and wood has been replaced by the shimmer of stainless steel. In the next room there are ten washbacks where the wort is fermented for 59 hours to 7.5% ABV. And then onwards to the still room, with its hot tangle of pipes, noise and humidity, a cathedral of distillation where three sets of three stills are hard at work. Business must be good as they operate 24 hours a day seven days a week, such is the demand for the clear new-make spirit produced.

In the cask store can be seen the Kentucky bourbon barrels and pipes that once contained port or sherry and into which the Bushmills spirit will be instilled. A display of glass-fronted barrels cleverly shows the angels' share, or devil's cut as they call it here – if only someone could develop a way of capturing the evaporating spirit. And then finally the visitor sees the clattering bottling and packaging lines where more than five million litres of whisky are bottled annually.

The standard tour ends in the visitor centre and shop and includes a tasting of whiskey. The Old Bushmills Distillery can be found at 2 Distillery Road, Bushmills, Co. Antrim, Northern Ireland BT57 8XH. The website is www.bushmills.com.

◄ **The still room provides the heartbeat of every distillery.**
(Bushmills)

▼ **Rolling out the barrel – a world shortage of barrels for whisky is forecast.** (Bushmills)

Craft distilling in Northern Ireland

Irish craft distilling is rising like a phoenix. Michael Morris's impressive plan, which will surely come to fruition, is to transform a dilapidated wing of the notorious Crumlin Road gaol in Belfast into a triple-still distillery – the first new distillery in the city for more than 80 years.

A tall ventilation chimney overlooks the austere but impressive former yard on the Crumlin Road gaol, where once the prisoners exercised, be they loyalists, republicans, suffragettes, murderers or ODCs (ordinary decent criminals).

'Go on, ask me why the ventilation chimney is so tall,' said Michael Morris, laughing. 'The Victorians built it twice as high as would have been needed as they thought crime was contagious and they didn't want anything released from the gaol to infect local people. The chimney is supposed to take away any evil spirits.'

▼ **An austere former prison is to become the home for a smart new distillery.** (Tim Hampson)

But Morris does more than talk a tall story – he talks a big game too and his spirit is certainly contagious. He believes that a new whiskey distillery will help regenerate the area and bring back into use more of the gaol buildings, which have been empty since 1995. While other wings of the gaol have already been renovated and opened for guided public tours, 'A' wing – the proposed home of the distillery – is currently a mess, with pigeons now living where prisoners used to be incarcerated.

Once Belfast was one of the biggest whisky cities in the distilling world, but Prohibition in the USA – the market for most of this *aqua vitae* – and Irish independence saw the end of it. A street directory from 1899 lists 18 distilleries and

bonded warehouses making and storing both pot-still and blended whiskey. Among the city's stars were the Avoniel, Cromac and Dunville distilleries – names that would have been known around the whisky-drinking world.

The scale of the operation was huge. The bonded warehouses of Dunville alone covered 11 acres and in the 1860s were home to more than 30,000 casks of whiskey, making the site the largest store of whiskey in Ireland. Today it has all gone: Dunville, the last of Belfast's distilleries established in the 19th century, closed in 1936.

Morris is one of Ireland's new wave of distillers. He is proud, ambitious and passionate about his products and their provenance. He works with Peter Lavery, Belfast's first lottery millionaire who, having won £10.2 million in May 1996, decided to invest some of his good fortune in founding the Belfast Distillery Company and introduced Titanic Irish Whiskey, a new brand of blended whiskey to commemorate the 100th anniversary of the *Titanic*, which was launched from one of the city's dockyards in 1911, when nearly 50% of all the whiskey produced in Ireland came from Belfast.

And while it is most unlikely that this scale of production will ever return to Belfast, Morris is adamant that distilling will return to the city. He explains that inside the old prison wing there will be a visitor centre and restaurant as part of the distillery, and the wing's former refectory – where guards once watched segregated republican and loyalist inmates from behind bullet-proof glass – will become a sampling room. Visitors will be able to sip glasses of Jailhouse poteen at the spot where, in 1993, a bomb smuggled into the gaol exploded.

Another of the new wave of distillers in Northern Ireland is Shane Braniff, who launched the Feckin whiskey brand in 2005 and then went on to found the Echlinville Distillery at Rubane, near Kircubbin, in 2012. This was the first distillery in Northern Ireland to be offered a licence (by HM Revenue and Customs) for more than 130 years.

'As our experience with Feckin has demonstrated,' states Braniff, 'demand for Irish whiskey is growing strongly in global markets. In fact, Irish whiskey is now the fastest-growing brown spirit worldwide. The success we are enjoying, particularly in the USA, has led us to invest in this new distillery.

'We are located on the Ards Peninsula, which boasts a unique micro-climate and is well suited to the production of whiskey. I think it may be the best whiskey-making location in the whole of Ireland and the rest of the UK. I do believe this gives us an edge.'

And Braniff is so confident of Echlinville's success that he has planted around 100 acres of malted barley to be used exclusively in his whiskey, giving not only full traceability on raw materials but also reducing the distillery's carbon footprint.

Clearly a bright new dawn awaits Northern Ireland's nascent whiskey industry.

▲ **Michael Morris has ambitious plans for whisky in Belfast.** (Tim Hampson)

▼ **A visitor centre is planned for the area where prisoners were once kept under lock and key.** (Tim Hampson)

Hops in whisky

The main difference between the washes made by distillers of whisky and brewers of beer is that the brewers add hops. But that is beginning to change and hops are being trialled by several of the new wave of craft whisky distillers. The hop is hip.

▲ **Hops are a key component of beer and are being trialled by some whisky makers.** (iStock)

Hops – the flowering cones of tall climbing bines – have been used for centuries to add bitterness to beer and to provide the essential preservative qualities that stop beers going bad. Traditionally whisky makers do not need hops because ageing in barrels adds flavour to the spirit and distillation increases the amount of alcohol, which preserves the drink. So for years brewers and distillers have worked away on their parallel but separate paths.

But now the two are starting to have a shared enthusiasm to talk about. In the brave new world of the craft-distilling industry, which is challenging the old orthodoxies, rules are meant to be broken. And why not? Whisky is traditionally flavoured by the oak from new barrels or the flavours of sherry or bourbon from old barrels, but why not bring to the process the new wave of flavoursome hop varieties, full of swirling citrus and other soft fruit notes, and widely used by many brewers? Rather than use an indifferent beer to distil from, why not start with a good, well-crafted hoppy one?

In America hopped whiskeys are being produced by Charbay in California, Corsair in Tennessee and New Holland Brewing in Michigan, while in the UK the Adnams distillery in Suffolk has been doing trials with hop-infused washes, using beer from its brewery.

The family-owned Charbay distillery was one of the early pioneers in the modern American artisan spirit-making movement, having begun distilling in the Napa Valley in 1983 with a wonderfully shaped copper alembic pot still. The heads

and tails of the hops are cut by hand and the process requires a lot of tasting by the distillers to ensure that only the best flavours make the final drink.

In 1999 Charbay experimented by distilling 20,000 gallons of pilsner to create 24 barrels of whiskey. European two-row barley, grown and malted in British Columbia, which has much more concentrated flavours than the more mainstream six-row barley, was used by the brewers of the pilsner and then the hops were added just before distillation to add the floral and spicy notes.

One of Charbay's latest releases is R5 Whiskey, which is distilled from Bear Republic's award-winning 7%-strength Racer 5 IPA beer. This beer is renowned for its upfront aromatic hops and its late, great, balanced dose of bittering hops and high-quality two-row barley, and its smooth, clean finish. Racer 5 is a beer for serious hop-heads as it has hop flavours in front, in the middle and in the finish, which is long, hoppy and citrus. It is heavily hopped with the four Cs – Chinook, Cascade, Columbus and Centennial – much admired by hop-heads. All of this is balanced by an underpinning rhythm of biscuit maltiness.

To make just 590 gallons of this whiskey, 6,000 gallons of Racer 5 beer was distilled in ten days in Charbay's 1,000-gallon still. The challenge was to see what characteristics would come through into the whiskey, half of which was unaged while the other half was aged in French oak for 29 months.

The time spent in oak brings this whiskey a light, golden, honey colour. The drink has the robust, warm and malty character one expects from a whiskey and even some swirls of smoke and honey. But there is an unusual melody, playing in the background, which slowly gets louder as taste buds become accustomed to the notes. And then the citrus hop flavours burst through the smokiness. It's a taste that could grow on people.

▶ **Californian distiller Charbay is at the forefront of craft spirit making.** (Charbay)

Beer from the whisky wood

Whisky is playing a part in a particular strand of innovation in brewing. Many brewers worldwide are now exploring the complexity of swirling flavours they can create by ageing beer in used spirit barrels.

Putting beer in wooden barrels, of course, is not a new thing. Before metals and plastics were used, wood was the common container for just about everything. And it was not uncommon for barrels to be used over and over again to transport everything from fresh water to fish.

Old whisky and bourbon barrels, in fact, were often used to store beer, but little attention was given to the myriad influences and flavours that would have shaped the beer inside. Beer aged in a barrel takes on the flavour of the wood, usually oak or chestnut, and also adopts the character of the barrel's previous inhabitant, which could be vanilla from bourbon casks or phenolic peaty notes from a barrel that once contained an Islay whisky. The wood can also add a wine-like complexity because of micro-organisms present in it.

However, the UK's tax authorities took a dim view of storing beer in old whisky casks – a practice they called 'grogging'. Tax officials outlawed grogging in 1835 as they feared brewers were doing it to add extra alcohol strength to beer without paying the necessary excise tax. Today, however, HM Revenue and Customs officials are much more understanding of the practice.

In the UK, Harviestoun Brewery in Clackmannanshire, Scotland, has been leading the way in barrel-ageing under the guidance of head brewer Stuart Cail. Following the success of Harviestoun's Ola Dubh ale, which the brewery makes by ageing its porter, Old Engine Oil, in Highland Park whisky barrels from the wild isles of Orkney, the company has launched a barrel-aged lager, Orach Slie, which is aged in casks from the Speyside distillery Glenfarclas that nestles in the rolling Speyside moors of Banffshire. In contrast to the punchy, dark Ola Dubh, Orach Slie is a much lighter, easy-going, slightly honeyed beer that reflects the softer, sweeter malts of Glenfarclas.

Thornbridge Brewery in Bakewell, Derbyshire, is another English brewer that has been experimenting with wood. By using an imperial stout as the base beer for ageing in three whisky casks, Thornbridge produced beers called Highland Whisky Reserve, Speyside Whisky Reserve and Islay Whisky Reserve. The array of aromas and flavours was beguiling: the Highland had oak, whisky and blackberry, Speyside was full of creamy malt, dark, burned fruit and roasted grain, while the Islay expression was, typically, rich with iodine and seaweed notes.

In London, Fuller's of Chiswick entered the oak-aged sector in style in 2008 with a Special Reserve No 1, matured for 500 days in 20-year-old bourbon casks acquired from Glenmorangie.

In the USA barrel-ageing is the current hot trend for its craft brewers. Chicago's Goose Island Beer Company led the way in 1992 when it released its first Bourbon County Brand Stout, a robust and gloriously chocolate-flavoured imperial stout.

But the practice could become a victim of its own success. The barrel-ageing style has become so popular that there is now a shortage of bourbon and whisky barrels…

▶ **Harviestoun has won many plaudits for its beers matured in old whisky and bourbon barrels.** (Cath Harries)

▶▶ **Storing beer in whisky casks has become a hot new trend.** (Fullers)

(Scotch Whisky Association)

The malt stars

Barley is the first of the building blocks for most whisky, but any grain – rye, maize, buckwheat or corn – can be used. The malting process provides a source of starch that can be converted into soluble, fermentable sugars, which in turn can be turned into alcohol.

'There is a quiet energy in here,' says Chris Garret, managing director of Warminster Maltings, as he thoughtfully examines a handful of three-day-old germinating barley. He carefully chooses one of the grains and rubs it to reveal the white, sweet goodness inside – liquid bread – while looking out over the expanse of germinating barley lying on one of the floors of the low-roofed maltings.

▶ **A quiet energy exudes from Warminster Maltings.** (Cath Harries)

▼ **Maltings can often be recognised from the outside by their rows of small ventilation windows, with seemingly insufficient space between the floor levels.** (Cath Harries)

▲ **Kilning produces malt of different colours which are prized by brewers. Distillers usually want lighter hues.** (Cath Harries)

▼ **Every batch of grain will be carefully tested and monitored in the laboratory.** (Cath Harries)

'You can just taste the sweetness and goodness in the malt,' he says, 'and those sugars are what the distiller is looking for. Without them we wouldn't have whisky.'

Distillers should regard barley varieties, Garret believes, just as wine producers think of grapes. He is concerned that many of the barleys being used nowadays are advantageous to farmers, as they are disease-resistant, high yielding and grow quickly, but that insufficient attention is given to the tastes and characteristics that different barleys bring to whisky.

Malting is a natural process that involves three stages: steeping, germination and kilning. Most malt in the world is made in large industrial malting plants, in batches as large as 500 tonnes, but at Warminster it is produced in traditional floor maltings – a small-scale, labour-intensive process – in ten-tonne batches. In a floor maltings germination literally takes place on the floor and kilning is a separate process, whereas in a modern maltings both processes usually occur in one vessel.

Malt from a floor maltings is highly regarded, not only by long-established whisky makers worldwide (indeed some still have their own maltings) but also by many of the new wave of craft distillers.

HOW BARLEY IS MALTED

(Beer Genie)

(All photos Cath Harries unless credited otherwise)

1 The story starts on the farm, with the planting, growing, harvesting and drying of the barley.

2 The dried grain arrives at a maltsters in bulk in large lorries. The first stage is to check if it is of a suitable quality and has the correct moisture content – about 12%.

3 Once inside the maltings, the barley will be wetted, a process known as 'steeping', in order to kickstart the germination of the grain.

4 Once steeping is completed, the grain is laid out on the long floor of the malthouse in a bed 15cm deep. The room soon heats up from the germinating grains, but the maltster does not want it too hot, as this will kill the grains, and controls the temperature by simply opening and closing the windows in the room.

5 It is hard graft working in a floor maltings. The turning and ploughing of the grain several times a day by hand untangles the rootlets, dissipates carbon dioxide and helps control the temperature.

6 When the grains have formed rootlets, after about three or four days, the germination has to be stopped. If the growth continues for too long, too much of the sugar-sweet goodness that the brewer needs will be gone.

7 The germinating grain, sometimes known as 'green malt', is moved to the floor below, where it is dried in a kiln for two days at temperatures in excess of 150°C to arrest the growth. Some distillers favour peat as a fuel for the kiln because this gives the malt an earthy, smoky flavour, as found in many Islay whiskies.

8 The grain is bagged, ready to go to the distiller. For some distillers the maltster will grind the malt into coarse flour so that it can be put straight into the mash or lauter tun.

9 Nothing is wasted. After kilning the rootlets of the germinated grain, known as culms, are removed. Culms are of no use to the distiller but are often used as animal feed because they are full of nutrients.

Distillation

Whisky is made by a simple, traditional process from three raw materials: malted grain (usually barley), water and yeast. Essentially the whisky maker produces a beer that is then distilled to create a clear, raw spirit.

The fundamental activity in a distillery is the process of distillation, whereby a relatively low-alcoholic-strength wash is converted – in a still – into a highly concentrated alcoholic liquid. To begin with, it is worth outlining the two types of still and how they work.

POT STILL

The pot still is the traditional batch process of distillation and is favoured by the makers of malt Scotch. The wash will be distilled twice in distinctive copper stills that act like large kettles – once in the wash still and once in the spirit safe. Compulsory in the UK, the spirit safe is a secure brass and glass box within which cutting takes place, without the stillman having any direct physical contact with the spirit. The safe is under the control of HM Revenue and Customs and from this moment the distillation is technically under its care until the tax (duty) is paid or the spirit is exported.

As the liquid is heated, alcohol vapours rise and pass over the head of the wash still and collect in a narrow tube known as the swan's neck before being guided though condensers, normally copper coils cooled by water, which turn it into a liquid again. The resulting spirit (around 30% ABV), known as the 'low wines', passes to the spirit still, where distillation is repeated. This creates a high-quality usable spirit (around 70% ABV), known as the 'middle' or 'heart of the run', which is then collected in the spirit safe.

The heads (called 'foreshots') and tails (called 'feints') have been removed. However, they do contain some drinkable ethanol as well as the potentially poisonous methanol and other unwanted toxins and flavour compounds. The heads and tails are added to the next batch of low wines and redistilled.

PATENT OR COFFEY STILL

Each still comprises two tall vertical columns, linked by pipes. One column is known as the analyser, the other the rectifier. Unlike batch production in a pot still, the process is

A VARIETY OF SPIRIT SAFES

a

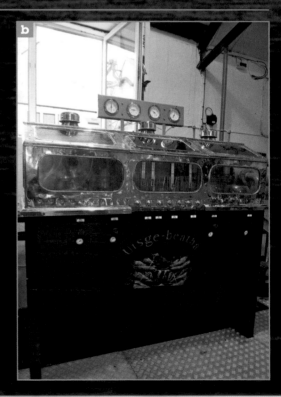

b

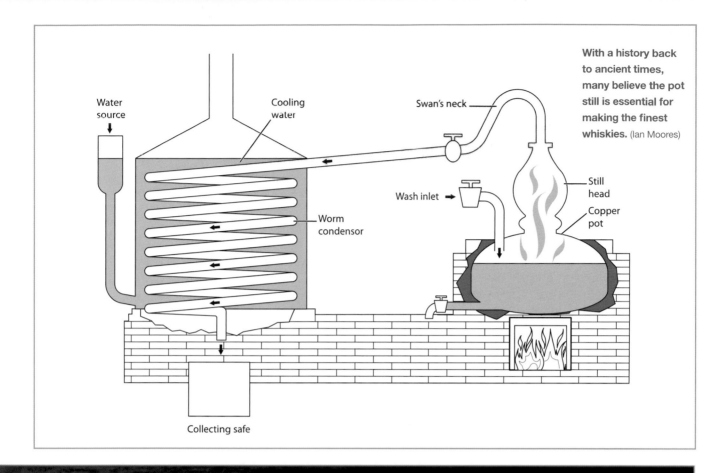

Water source

Cooling water

Swan's neck

With a history back to ancient times, many believe the pot still is essential for making the finest whiskies. (Ian Moores)

Still head

Wash inlet

Copper pot

Worm condensor

Collecting safe

α **Oban: A spirit safe is an object functional beauty. Oban's is no exception.** (Cath Harries)

b **Bowmore: The first and the last fraction (foreshots and feints) are recycled back for redistillation, through the spirit safe.** (Cath Harries)

c **Glenfarclas: The middle cut goes via the spirit safe into the spirit store to be filled into barrels.** (Bowmore)

d **Bruichladdich: Originally the spirit safe was installed by the exciseman to stop new make spirit being siphoned off.** (Cath Harries)

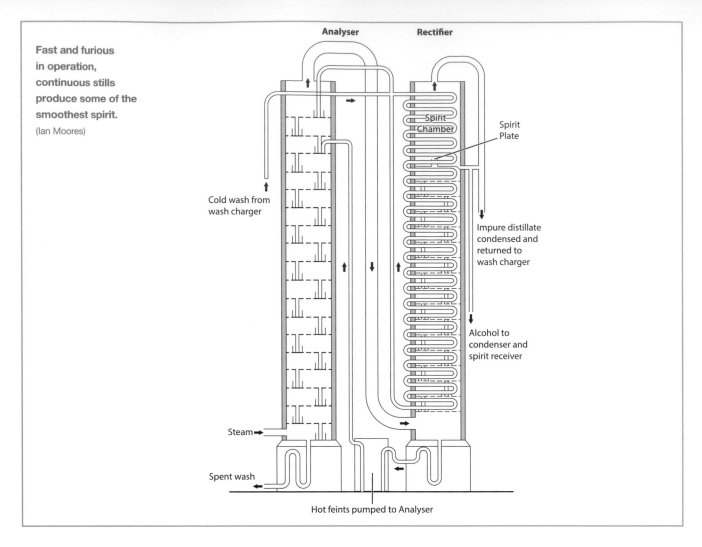

**Fast and furious
in operation,
continuous stills
produce some of the
smoothest spirit.**

(Ian Moores)

Analyser

Rectifier

Spirit Chamber

Spirit Plate

Cold wash from wash charger

Impure distillate condensed and returned to wash charger

Alcohol to condenser and spirit receiver

Steam

Spent wash

Hot feints pumped to Analyser

continuous; the Coffey is the most commonly used continuous still, but there are others.

The wash is pumped in at the top of the rectifier, where it flows down coils and is warmed by the heat of vapours rising up the still. Once heated, the wash enters the top of the analyser and descends through perforated plates. As it descends, low-pressure steam rises up the analyser and extracts alcohol vapours, which are taken back to the bottom of the rectifier.

The alcohol vapours then start to rise in the rectifier and are gradually condensed by the cool wash coils, with the spirit extracted from the rectifier column. The distillation is a continuous process, with the different vapours condensed and drawn off from the still at different alcoholic strengths, depending on where the spirit plates are positioned.

The heavier fusel oils and congeners stripped from the wash by the initial distillation in the analyser are not volatile enough to reach the upper plates of the rectifier. They drop to the bottom of the column, where they are drawn off and pumped back into the analyser with the wash.

In this way only very alcohol-rich vapour can reach the

top half of the rectifier. Each plate in the rectifier is like a mini distillation chamber, with the alcoholic percentage of the liquid/vapour mix increasing as it gets further up the column. Depending on which plate the spirit is drawn from, alcohol produced in this way can be rectified up to a strength of around 96.4% ABV.

Harmful high alcohols are drawn off at the very top of the rectifier, where only they can reach, and are condensed and recycled into the analyser. Just below this point the 'heart of the run' alcoholic vapour is drawn off, condensed and sent to the spirit receivers.

The distilled liquid has a higher purity and alcohol level than comes from a pot still, and only goes through one distillation. Many experts say the spirit created in a continuous still has a more neutral flavour than one created in a pot still.

In all cases where a spirit is being made the distillate is separated into three components: the 'heads' (the most volatile components), the 'heart of the run' (the drinkable fraction) and the 'tails' (the least volatile components). The heads and tails will not be used as they contain toxic compounds but they will be redistilled.

FOUR STEPS FROM GRAIN TO GLASS

1 The dried malt is ground in a mill. The resultant crushed grain is known as grist.

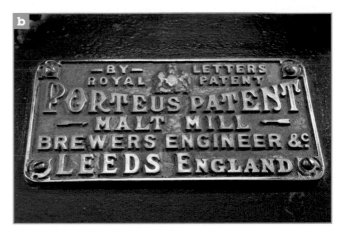

a Many Scottish distilleries still use 100-year-old Bobby mills, but most use the more-modern Porteus. (Cath Harries)

b English engineering at its best – Porteus mills are tireless workhorses. (Cath Harries)

c The mill produces a grist of cracked grain and flour. (Cath Harries)

d The quality of the grist is tested by passing it through a sieve to see if it has the correct amount of coarse, medium and fine particles. (Cath Harries)

2 The grist is mixed with hot water in a mash tun, which is also known as a lauter tun. Sugars from the crushed grain dissolve in the water, creating a sugary liquid known as wort. It is this liquid that is turned into one containing alcohol. The sweet wort is then drained off the now-spent grain.

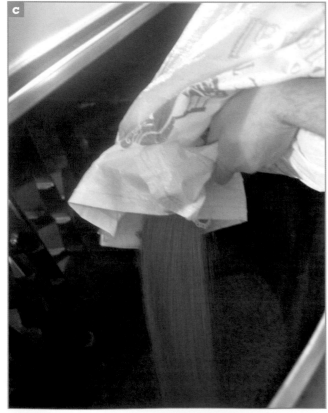

a **Mash tuns will often have a hatch to allow the removal of spent grains.** (Cath Harries)

b **There is a lot of manual handling in a small distillery.** (Cath Harries)

c **When the water has been heated to the correct temperature, the grain is poured in.** (Cath Harries)

d **Inside the mash tun is a series of paddles for stirring the mash.** (Cath Harries)

A VARIETY OF MASH TUNS

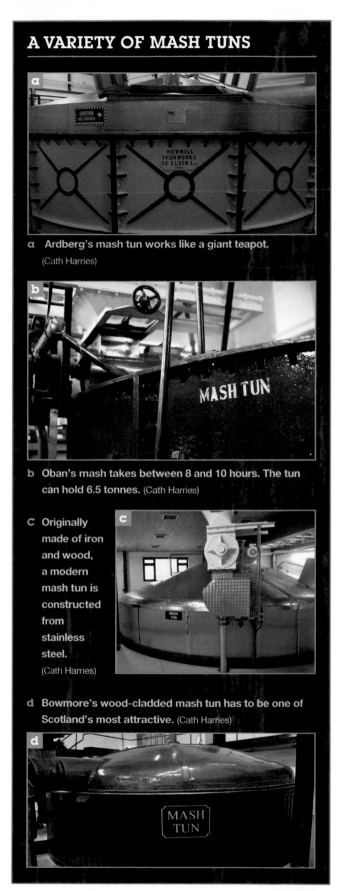

a   Ardberg's mash tun works like a giant teapot.
(Cath Harries)

b   Oban's mash takes between 8 and 10 hours. The tun can hold 6.5 tonnes. (Cath Harries)

c   Originally made of iron and wood, a modern mash tun is constructed from stainless steel.
(Cath Harries)

d   Bowmore's wood-cladded mash tun has to be one of Scotland's most attractive. (Cath Harries)

e   Great care is taken to ensure the mash doesn't set into a thick porridge.
(Cath Harries)

f   Temperature is crucial to ensuring the maximum extract of fermentable sugars from the grist.
(Cath Harries)

g   Once the mash is finished the spent grain goes for animal feed.
(Cath Harries)

3 The wort passes into a large vessel called a washback. Yeast is added to the wort and the magic of transforming fermentable sugars into alcohol begins. As part of its lifecycle, yeast feeds off the sugars in the wort, turning them into alcohol and carbon dioxide. The alcoholic liquid, known as the wash, has a strength of about 8% ABV.

a Once fermentation begins in a washback, bubbles of carbon dioxide rise to the top. (Cath Harries)

b Liquid is drawn out of the mash tun so the fermentable sugars can be measured. (Cath Harries)

c Measurement and record keeping are a vital part of whisky making. (Cath Harries)

d The wash might not be much to look at, but it's an essential phase on the way to making a whisky. (Cath Harries)

4 The wash is now distilled in the still. During distillation the relatively low-alcoholic-strength wash is converted into a highly concentrated alcoholic liquid. The concentration is achieved by separating the different components – or 'fractions' – in the wash. This separation is achieved because each of the fractions boils at a different temperature and turns into vapour. The vapours can be turned back into liquid by condensing them. The broader the range of vapours that are condensed, the more flavour the raw spirit will have. Drinkable alcohol, known as ethanol, boils at 78.5°C, so if the wash is heated to this temperature the 'potable' (drinkable alcohol) is boiled off, leaving behind the other constituents – mostly water but also congeners and fusel oils.

a   Visually attractive, beguiling and highly engineered, stills exude character. This one is called Matilda. (Cath Harries)

b   A porthole in the pot still allows the process to be visually monitored. (Cath Harries)

c   Temperature control of the still is vital for the production of fine spirit. (Cath Harries)

d   Once the stillman is happy, the middle cut is run off into a spirit store. (Cath Harries)

e The first distillation pass through a pot still produces the low wines. (Cath Harries)

f Full of flavour and character, the final spirit from a pot still is not as strong as that from a Coffey. (Cath Harries)

g Every stage of distillation needs to be closely monitored. (Cath Harries)

h Before maturation in wooden barrels, whisky is a clear spirit. (Cath Harries)

i Prior to filling, the bung needs to be removed from a wooden cask. (Cath Harries)

j Once filled, the barrel's bung needs to be tapped back into place. (Cath Harries)

STILL LIFE

a Bruichladdich: At Bruichladdich on Islay, Ugly Betty is used to make an award-winning 22 botanical gin. (Cath Harries)

b Ardbeg: Spirit from Ardbeg's still was once sent to the International Space Station to study how it was affected by zero gravity. (Cath Harries)

c Bannahabhain: Bunnahabhain stills produce some of Islay's unpeated malts. (Cath Harries)

d Oban: Oban has only two stills, making it one of the smallest distillers in Scotland. (Cath Harries)

e Glenburgie: Two of the three pairs of hard-working stills operating at the Glenburgie distillery. (Pernod Ricard)

Wood you believe it?

Wood is much more than a benign storage container – it is the very essence of a whisky's character. Wood – not water, barley or yeast – has the greatest influence on the flavour and colour of whisky. In fact it is estimated that upwards of 60% of a whisky's flavour comes from this interaction of spirit and wood.

The discovery of the part played by wood was probably accidental. Newly made spirit had to be put into something, and there was a time when wooden barrels were the workhorses for carrying pretty much everything from water to gunpowder.

Although the influence of wood is such an important part of the whisky-making process, it is the least understood.

The wood that was used to build seagoing vessels for generations, oak, is also the wood of choice for whisky making, for both legal and practical reasons. In most countries where whisky is made there are laws specifying that it must be matured in a wooden barrel of a certain size for a specific period of time. For example, for any spirit to be called Scotch it has been made mandatory since 1915 that it is not only distilled and matured in Scotland but also that it has been aged in oak barrels for at least three years, although in

◄ **The evaporation of whisky from a cask, the angels' share, can clearly be seen at Jameson's Middle museum.** (Jameson)

◀ **The waiting game. Outside many distilleries can be found a store of used bourbon barrels ready to be filled with spirit.** (Glenfarclas)

practice most will have been matured for much longer. In the US bourbon must be matured in oak for at least two years and a new barrel must be used each time.

Oak is a strong, slow-growing tree and the wood is sufficiently malleable to be shaped into casks. The resulting casks remove impurities and undesirable flavours such as sulphur from the spirit. In addition, oak is rich in its own flavour compounds that are easily released by charring or toasting the wood, giving the spirit – especially bourbon – pleasant vanilla, spicy and toasted flavours.

Wood is also porous enough to allow oxygen and other molecules to pass through to perform beneficial oxidation reactions. The different alcohols and aldehydes are oxidised, and acids react with ethanol to form esters – which are some of the most gloriously aromatic of whisky flavour compounds.

Oak also allows the casks to respire and release the angels' share, or devil's cut, by evaporation into the atmosphere. In addition compounds within the oak itself react with compounds in the spirit, helping to develop it into a full-flavoured whisky. And it is the timber that gives whisky its golden hue, releasing chemicals called melanoidins. Added to this may be coloration from previous alcohol in the cask.

▲ **Casks have a profound influence on whisky – at some distilleries visitors can experience the flavours from different barrels.** (Cath Harries)

◣ **The source of the wood from which the cask is made can also influence a whisky's character.** (Cath Harries)

▼ **It takes time, but slowly whisky's colour changes from a clear spirit to a darker, entrancing liquid.** (Cath Harries)

OZARK MOUNTAIN RANGE, USA
BOURBON CASKS
AMERICAN WHITE OAK

JEREZ REGION, SPAIN
SHERRY CASKS
EUROPEAN OAK

LIMOUSIN, FRANCE
COGNAC AND WINE CASKS
FRENCH LIMOUSIN

THE INFLUENCE OF THE CASK

CASK
EUROPEAN SHERRY

0 YEARS   3 YEARS   10 YEARS   12 YEARS

CASK
AMERICAN BOURBON

0 YEARS   3 YEARS   10 YEARS   12 YEARS

CASK
REFILL

0 YEARS   3 YEARS   10 YEARS   12 YEARS

▲ At Adnams, virgin oak barrels are used to mature the whisky.
(Cath Harries)

▼ Amrut oak barrels are charred before they are filled with spirit.
(Amrut)

The size of cask determines how quickly reactions occur, as maturation will be quicker when more whisky is in contact with the wood. Some of the new wave of producers in countries without a whisky-making tradition put the spirit into smaller barrels, so that a greater proportion of the liquid comes into contact with the wood – and the containers are turned frequently to ensure maximum interaction between oak and spirit.

The effects of oak on whisky spirit, therefore, are profound. But to the mix is added a further complication – what was in the oak barrel before the spirit is put in. American whiskey has to use virgin oak and so its flavours and colours come wholly from the charred interior surface; lightly burning the wood releases lignin and this unlocks aromatic, coconut-flavoured aldehydes in the spirit.

In Scotland and Ireland, whisky makers can use new wood, but the resulting tannin and spicy flavours can overwhelm the drink. Often the casks, therefore, have been used previously for other drinks – traditionally sherry and, since the 1960s, bourbon. Conventionally there are three main types of cask for whisky making – bourbon oak casks and sherry casks of European oak or American oak.

The differences between *Quercus Robur* (European oak) and *Quercus Alba* (American oak) are profound. The tighter, more compact grain of the slower-growing European variety gives its flavour to the spirit in a more leisurely way. American

▲ A Japanese oak, Mizunara oak, is said to bring vanilla flavours to whisky. (Cath Harries)

oak tends to have more of the compounds called lactones, which give more vanilla tastes and the coconut flavour often present in bourbon.

Wood grown in less familiar countries can add to the majesty of a whisky's flavour profile. A Japanese whisky stored in Mizunara oak, which has been used since the 1930s and is extremely porous, will be high in vanilla, fresh fruit and blossom flavours. Russian oak is said to impart more aromatic flavours. Expect whisky matured in Spanish oak to have spicy and soaring floral flavours.

Added to this are the flavours that emanate from previous occupants of a barrel – bourbon, red wine, white wine, port, rum or sherry. Further factors are how often and for how long a barrel has been used to store whisky. And then there is the fact that many whiskies are matured in more than one barrel, spending time first in an ex-bourbon barrel before being transferred to a port or sherry type.

You can see that the part played by wood in making a whisky is very complex.

▶ Rolling out the barrel – distillers often move filled barrels to a different store. (Cath Harries)

Whisky blending

Blended or single-malt – which is better? It is a question that many whisky fans ask, and too many believe that a single-malt is a superior product to a blend. Things are not that simple: these two terms only tell you how the whisky has been made – they are not a reference to its quality.

The term 'blended' simply means that a whisky has been mixed together from a minimum of one single-malt whisky (made using malted barley from one distillery) and one unmalted grain whisky. Without blending – the art of mixing different whiskies together – whisky might not have become so renowned worldwide.

Blending whisky is all about balance – combining whiskies, often with markedly different characters, into a harmonious, drinkable ensemble. In assessing whiskies, the nose is the blender's most valuable tool.

A combination of a change in the law, advances in technology and increased demand for whisky saw blending become widely adopted more than 150 years ago, having been pioneered by Andrew Usher in Edinburgh. In 1823 a new Excise Act loosened the regulations for making whisky in Scotland and also reduced duties. It was a transformational moment, along with the perfection by Aeneas Coffey of the design of a

continuous still, or patent still, to produce a milder-flavoured grain whisky that could be produced in greater quantities and more cheaply than single-malt whisky, using unmalted grain.

Only malt whisky existed before the patent stills appeared, and, indeed, whisky was very seldom known outside Scotland or Ireland.

Having the two distillation processes allowed whisky makers to start blending malt and grain whiskies to produce a drink that was milder, more consistent and of greater popular appeal, in particular to French drinkers of brandy who were deprived of their favourite tipple in the 1860s because the *Phylloxera* bug's swift advance through French vineyards restricted the production of port and cognac.

A blended whisky can be made by combining any number of single-malt whiskies and grain whiskies to create the required flavour and characteristics. These whiskies can be from different distilleries and of different ages. Indeed some

◀ **Every barrel of whisky will be regularly opened and its contents evaluated.** (Cath Harries)

▶ **Every cask of whisky will have its own profound character.** (Cath Harries)

▼ **The skill of the whisky maker is in being able to assess the quality of each cask.** (Cath Harries)

▲ **A good sense of smell is crucial to the best whisky makers.**
(Cath Harries)

producers do not distil at all but buy in whiskies to make their blends.

Blends are a careful combination of art, craft and science, and most distilleries and individual blenders have their own secret recipes. Typically 20–25 whiskies are used in a blend, with around 20–50% of those being single-malt whiskies, but some blends use more than 50 whiskies.

Professional blenders often use three terms to describe the component malts in their blends:

■ **Packers** These are the workhorses that can make up half the malt content of the blend and add bulk to it. Blenders choose them to combine well with the other malts, but without adding a great deal in terms of final flavour.
■ **Core malts** These tend to define the overall character of the finished blend.
■ **Top dressers** These malts are high-quality whiskies that are used for adding depth and top notes to the mix.

The core malts of a blended Scotch are often constructed around a mix of Speyside malts, which may make up

approximately 50% of the malt total, and perhaps some 10% of Highland and Islay malts to bring complexity to the party, although the most powerful of the phenolic-flavoured Islays rarely contribute more than 2% of the malt total, to avoid their effect becoming overpowering.

The remaining 40% of the blend comprises the packers. Often grain whisky, these provide the supporting chorus, and rarely step to the front of the stage.

In a commercial distillery or blenders, once a recipe has been decided upon, the component whiskies are mixed together in a large steel vessel or vat, and then de-ionised water will often be added to reduce the alcohol content to a bottling strength of 40–43% ABV.

Usually the blend is then filtered to remove any larger particles that were present in the wooden casks. Some whiskies are chill-filtered, during which the temperature of the spirit is reduced to around 0°C and it is passed through an ultra-fine filter to remove particles that may cause it to go cloudy or dull when water or ice is added. Occasionally a small quantity of caramel may be added to ensure colour consistency of a blend.

Each blender has its own way of doing it. At Whyte & Mackay, for example, the component malts are stored in wood for several months before being blended with the grain whisky, and the resultant blend is matured for a further period before bottling.

RECREATING A 100-YEAR-OLD BLEND

At William Grant, which was established in 1887, Brian Kinsman is only the sixth master blender in the company's entire history. In 2012 he replicated the original Stand Fast blend – named after the Grant family's clan motto – of 1912 and produced 100 bottles by using whiskies similar to those found in the original blend.

Company archivist Paul Kendall discovered the details in a recipe book that was thought to have been lost. It listed quantities and details of the first ever version of William Grant's blend, which was recorded in the book on 11 June 1912 and named as Blend No.1. Kinsman used his skills to interpret the old records to recreate the Speyside whisky, which has undoubtedly evolved over the years as distilleries have come and gone.

'As a master blender we learn how to make whisky by knowledge handed down in person from one master blender to the next,' said Kinsman. 'This is why it takes around a decade of training to take on the title.'

Making a great blended whisky is a complex combination of precise science and practised judgement. For example, the flavours of whisky's natural ingredients vary from year to year, so Kinsman constantly uses his skill and experience to balance out seasonal changes and produce a consistent, distinctive taste.

According to Kinsman, the task should have been easy enough as all the whiskies – 18 of them – were clearly itemised in the book together with their ages and the proportions used.

▲ **Glenfarclas brand ambassador George Grant, whose family have run a distillery for six generations, needs a good nose.**
(Cath Harries)

However, life is not that simple. Some of the distilleries William Grant worked with in 1912 have long since closed, and back then whiskies would have been slightly smokier as the casks used for maturation generally would have been ex-sherry casks.

So, like all recreations, significant brushes of artistic licence were used to complete the project. Older whiskies were used, for example, rather than the two-year-olds specified in the original recipe; in any case it is illegal today to call a two-year-old spirit a whisky.

Kinsman started with a firm foundation of grain whisky, which was to make up 60% of the blend. After individual nosing, seven grain whiskies of various vintages went into the mix. Typically these whiskies are not available to the general public and are much sought-after by blenders: two youngish whiskies came from North British and two more came from Port Dundas (including a 19-year-old), and there was a 24-year-old Cambus, a 26-year-old Caledonian and a five-year-old Girvan (which had been stored in ex-sherry casks).

Then, separately, the 11 different aged single-malt whiskies, including two peaty ones, were blended after separate nosing. The single-malt array comprised six Balvenies, four Glenfiddichs and a nine-year-old Highland Park.

After separate tastings the grains and malts were then bought together. Typically this is done in small quantities in laboratory conditions, before larger quantities are mixed together in vats.

Once the selected whiskies were blended, they were left to marry before bottling. During this time, the final flavours and aromas emerged, creating greater depth and consistency of flavour.

And the final challenge was bottling. Stand Fast, like the majority of today's whiskies, was bottled at 40% ABV. In order to prevent the natural haze that usually forms in whiskies at that strength, modern whiskies often undergo a process known as chilled filtration, but back in 1912 reducing the temperature of a whisky before bottling was not common practice, if done at all. Instead, it is likely that whisky would have been filtered using egg white. If egg white is mixed with whisky, the compounds that some people consider unsightly – because they make whisky cloudy – stick to the albumen and can be filtered out with relative ease.

Does the 'new' Stand Fast taste the same as its 1912 forebear? We will never know, of course, but it is a vivid example of the consummate skill needed to blend a quality whisky.

Blending at home

One way to learn more about whisky is to blend your own at home. Yes, you can create your own unique whisky using one of the home blend kits that are available and then, if you like it, you can have it made up for yourself and bottled.

As well as being a bit of fun, do-it-yourself blending is a great way to learn about different whiskies and hone your tasting and nosing skills. To start you off, there are companies that market home-blending kits, such as the one featured here from Master of Malt (www.masterofmalt.com/blend-your-own-whisky).

Inside a typical kit you will find:

- **Base whiskies** Two single base whiskies and two mild malts.
- **Mid-range malts** A Speyside (sherry-matured), Highland, Islay and Lowland.
- **Cherries for the top of the cake** An old sherry-matured Highland and an old grain whisky.

Fools rush in, but patience will be rewarded. The temptation is to get going immediately and just start pouring, but planning, patience, time and a trained nose are essential to get the most out of blending.

Decide what character of blend you want to create – something screamingly loud and heavily peated or a more softly spoken dram? Are you looking for a Ferrari or a Bentley?

Like all good buildings, it is important to start with solid foundations. So begin at the bottom with the base whiskies and gradually build your blend, then go on to add the mid-range malts, and finally use the 'cherries' for the final flourish.

Less is more: rather than simply pouring out everything in the kit, confine yourself to a few carefully selected whiskies so that each can shine and contribute. Over-exuberance is the road to madness!

Use peat in moderation: peated whiskies can easily overpower a blend, so always use less than you think you need, even if you are going for a peaty dram.

As a general rule grain whiskies temper the more unruly malts, acting as the calming peacemakers in the blend. Forget the refrain that pot-stilled whiskies are the only good whiskies.

HOW TO MAKE THE HAYNES BLEND

Equipment (as provided in the kit)
- 3ml pipette
- 1ml pipette
- 10ml measuring cylinder
- 25ml measuring cylinder
- 100ml conical flask
- Tasting glass

(All photos: Cath Harries)

1 Take stock of the different whiskies in the kit, as follows:

- 3cl Single Grain Base (x2)
- 3cl Malt Base
- 3cl Speyside Single Malt (sherry-matured)
- 3cl Highland Single Malt
- 3cl Islay Single Malt
- 3cl Lowland Single Malt
- 3cl Old Highland Single Malt (sherry-finished)
- 3cl Old Speyside Single Malt
- 3cl Very, Very Old Grain
- 3cl Very Old Islay Single Malt

2 Open up the bottles and nose each one. What are their attributes? It is best to make written notes of your judgements rather than rely on memory. Take your time – and repeat the nosing as you need to.

3 For the base use the Single Grain and Malt Bases. These will form the power train for your blend. Malt will provide complexity, while the grain is likely to provide the bulk and a calming influence on its whisky cousin. For the Haynes Blend 33% Single Grain Base and 23% Very, Very Old Grain were used, giving a total of 56% grain. Of course, some blends have considerably more than this, and equally, with such a fantastic choice of single-malts, you may wish to have a lot less.

4 Then add the malts. Be sure only to add tiny amounts at a time, using a pipette. Give the process time: some blends take a little while for their best attributes to come to the fore.

5 Carefully mix your finished blend. For the Haynes Blend, the chosen malt constituents were:
- 15% Malt Base
- 7% Speyside (sherry-matured)
- 15% Lowland Single Malt
- 6% Old Highland Single Malt (sherry-finished)
- 1% Very Old Islay Single Malt

6 The proof is in the glass: carefully pour your blend into your mixing glass.

7 First nose your blend. My verdict of the Haynes Blend: vanilla, some butter and hints of gee; sweet baked bread and a suggestion of fresh dough. Then sip.

8 What is it like? Palate: crisp with hints of cereal; a smooth creaminess gives way to hints of pepper and spice. Finish: fresh and relatively short with a swirl of Islay smoke. The verdict: appealing and delightfully 'moreish'.

GLOSSARY

ABV (alcohol by volume) The alcohol strength of a whisky measured as a percentage in relation to the liquid as a whole: 40% ABV is equal to 40% alcohol and 60% water.

Age The number of years a whisky has been maturing in the cask.

Age statement Labels with an age statement such as '10-year-old' indicate the youngest component whisky in a blend; some of it could be much older.

Ageing Whisky gets its individual character by maturing inside an oak cask for a period of time. For whisky from Scotland this must be at least three years, whereas bourbon can be ready in two years. Once bottled, no further maturation takes place – unlike some wines or bottled conditioned beers – but the taste can change over time.

American oak This hard wood is ideal for making casks and often contributes tannin flavours to the whisky. The staves are usually thicker than those used for casks of European oak and this means that the angels' share is less.

Angels' share The stuff of legend, this is the alcohol lost due to evaporation during maturation in the cask. In a Scottish distillery the loss could amount to around 2% each year, but losses are often higher in hotter climates, such as in India and the USA.

Barrel A generic term for a cask; in the UK a barrel has a specific capacity of 36 Imperial gallons (164 litres).

Beading A rough-and-ready method used to tell the alcoholic strength of a whisky. When a bottle is shaken, bubbles or beads appear – the longer lasting the bubbles, the greater the alcohol content of the whisky. To see the difference, try this with a cask-strength whisky and a blend or single-malt.

Blending This is the craft of taking a number of different whiskies – just two or three, or as many as 50 – to produce a whisky with a defined and recognisable character. Combining malt whisky with grain whisky proved to be a turning point for the Scottish whisky industry and saw demand grow first in England and then worldwide.

Bourbon The classic US style of whiskey, which by law must be made from a mash of at least 51% corn grain. The spirit is matured in new, white oak barrels that have previously been charred, or thermally degraded.

(Buffalo Trace)

(Cath Harries)

Bourbon, small batch Many US distillers have developed the concept of small-batch unblended Bourbons – an idea inspired by the appeal of single-malt Scotch whiskies.

Brewing The process that follows malting in the production of malt whisky, and consists of mashing and fermentation; in Irish distilling, brewing is usually taken to mean just mashing, with fermentation being considered a separate, subsequent operation.

Butt The type of large cask regularly used by the whisky industry for maturation purposes; a butt contains 108 Imperial gallons (491 litres), twice the amount of a hogshead.

Campbeltown The smallest of the generally recognised Scotch whisky regions, located on the Kintyre peninsula in Argyllshire.

Cask A wooden barrel, usually made of oak, in which whisky is stored in order to mature. It is normal to age Scotch in barrels originally used for bourbon (American oak) or sherry (European oak) to impart character to the whisky.

Cask strength When whisky is ready for bottling, it is usually around 50–60% ABV, and water is then added to bring it down to around 40% ABV. However, some whiskies are bottled at their original cask strength and sold as special editions.

Charring As part of the cask-making process, the inside of a new barrel is briefly burned, the resultant charring adding to the flavour of the whisky.

Chill filtration Whisky is often chilled before bottling to remove the natural substances that can cause the spirit to become cloudy if stored at low temperature or diluted with water. However, there is a growing trend towards selling unfiltered whisky because it is believed that the presence of certain chemical compounds called congeners (see below) adds to the complexity of the drink.

Clearic New-make spirit, straight from the still. Clear in colour and high in strength, this was a popular drink with distillery workers when the practice of dramming (see following page) was common.

Coffey still Patented in 1830 by Aeneas Coffey, a former Irish Inspector-General of Excise, the Coffey still revolutionised whisky making. Also known as the column, continuous or patent still, it allows large quantities of spirit to be distilled much more quickly than in the traditional pot still. Originally it comprised two tall columns, the first being the analyser, which separates the spirit from the wash, while the second, known as the rectifier, further concentrates the spirit.

Condenser A heat exchanger that condenses vaporised alcohol into its liquid form to be collected via the low wines or spirits safe.

Congeners Chemical compounds produced during fermentation and maturation. Congeners include esters, aldehydes, acids and higher alcohols. These are impurities in the whisky, but they give its flavour. Too much or too little of these congeners would make a whisky undrinkable.

Continuous distillation Using a long column or Coffey still, the wash is passed over steam under high pressure; continuous distillation produces higher-strength alcohol than a pot still.

(Cath Harries)

Cooper Someone who makes a wooden barrel; once the craft of coopering was widespread, but today it is really only kept alive by the whisky industry.

Corn The cereal at the heart of most North American whiskies, notably bourbon. Corn whiskey is also a term for a type of US whiskey that has strong associations with 'moonshining'.

Cut point During distillation, the condensed vapour is separated into three parts or 'cuts'. The first cut is called the 'heads' or 'foreshots', which contain a high proportion of toxic methanol and acetone, and other liquids with low boiling points. As the temperature increases, the next cut is called the 'heart of the run' and this is the spirit that will evolve into whisky. The third cut is called the 'tails' or 'feints', and includes a host of aromatic compounds that give desirable flavours.

Cutting During distillation, the stillman, or stillhouse computer programme, cuts from collecting foreshots to the middle cut or heart of the run, before then cutting back to collect feints. Cut points are crucial to the character of the spirit produced, and every distillery has its own formula for them, based on alcoholic strength and/or timescale.

Distillation The separation of alcohol from the fermented wash; whisky can be distilled twice or even three times.

Draff The name for the spent grain after fermentation; draff can be used as a nutritious food for cattle or pigs.

Dram The traditional Scotch whisky measure, although it has no specific size; often affectionately referred to as a 'wee dram'.

Dramming In an era before drink/drive laws and health and safety legislation, workers would enjoy dramming – drinking spirit straight from casks during their working day.

Dunnage A traditional stone or brick warehouse for storing whisky casks, ideally with an earth-covered floor; casks are stacked no more than three high on ash runners.

Expression A distiller may make several different versions of its whiskies available, often with different age statements or with different finishes – each of these is known as an expression.

Feints The third and final fraction (part) of the distilled alcohol from the spirit still; the feints are mostly water and are redistilled.

Fermentation The process of turning sugar into alcohol. In whisky production, yeast is added to sweet, unfermented wort in a washback, and the magic of fermentation begins.

Fillings The term used for newly distilled spirit that has been put into casks. A spirit cannot be called Scotch until it has been allowed to mature for at least three years in Scotland.

Finish The final element of nosing and tasting a whisky – the finish describes the duration of flavours lingering in the mouth and throat after swallowing.

Finishing The term for taking a malt whisky that has matured in an original cask and putting it in a second cask – usually one previously used for port, Madeira, Burgundy or sherry

– for around six months. This gives the whisky a different complexity and depth, with a broader array of aromas.

Foreshot The first fraction (part) of the distilled alcohol from the spirit still; foreshots, which are about 80% ABV, are returned to the spirit still to be redistilled.

Grain whisky A whisky made from unmalted barley, wheat or corn.

Green malt At the point when germination is halted during malting, the barley is referred to as green malt.

Grist Malt barley and other cereals are cracked in a large mill before they are mixed with warm water in the mash tun; the grains are literally grist for the mill.

Heart of the run The second fraction (part) of the distilled alcohol from the spirit still, between the foreshot and the feints; the 'heart of the run' is what the distiller is looking for and it is collected, ready to be matured into whisky.

Highland malts These are what it says on the bottles – whiskies from the Scottish Highlands. This area is defined as the part of Scotland north of a theoretical line between Greenock on the Firth of Clyde in the west and Dundee in the east. Although geographically part of the Highland region, Speyside is usually considered to merit its own classification.

Hogshead A large cask of 54 Imperial gallons (245 litres) used for maturing whisky.

Irish whiskey By law, Irish whiskey has to be distilled and matured in Ireland for a minimum of three years.

Island malts Whiskies from distilleries on the islands of Scotland; these are often defined by peaty flavours derived from the production process, but not all Scottish island whiskies contain such flavours.

Jigger The name for an illicit distillery; it is also a US spirit measure, normally of 1½ US fluid ounces (44 millilitres).

Kiln As part of the malting process, the germinating barley is dried in a kiln to arrest germination.

Low wines The name given to the first distillation from a pot still. It forms the raw material of the second distillation, which happens in the spirit still. The feints and foreshots are added to the low wines when the spirit still is charged.

Lowland malts The collective name for whiskies from Scotland's Lowlands. These tend to be lighter in both colour and body than whisky from the Highlands, and fresh, floral and cereal aromas can often be detected.

Lyne arm The pipe from the pot still where the spirit vapours are transferred, to be condensed back into a liquid. The angle of the pipe is believed to influence the character of the whisky and contributes to giving it a light or heavy body.

Malt whisky This indicates that the raw material is 100% malted barley, fermented with yeast and distilled in a pot still.

Malting The process by which barley grains are allowed to germinate by soaking in water before being dried in a kiln; the process of germination converts starch in the grain to fermentable sugars.

(Cath Harries)

Mash tun The large vessel in which the mashing process takes place; it is usually circular and made from cast iron, stainless steel, wood or copper.

Mashing Similar to making a large pot of tea, the addition of hot water to the grist (coarsely ground grain) releases the sweet goodness in the grain into the liquid, which can then be fermented to make alcohol.

Maturation The process in which the whisky ages in its cask, acquiring its character. A complex exchange, often referred to as a 'conversation', takes place between the spirit and the cask's wood, which creates the flavours, strength and balance.

Middle cut The most pure and desirable spirit collected during distillation, it is also known as the 'heart of the run' and goes on to be matured as whisky.

Moonshine A term from the USA during the Prohibition era, when, to avoid detection, distillers worked at night in secret locations. It is a description loved by today's new wave of craft distillers, especially those who make unaged corn distillations.

New make The clear, alcoholic liquid that comes off a still.

Nosing In terms of appreciating taste, one's nose is far more powerful than the taste buds on one's tongue. Time spent sniffing a whisky opens up a new world of tastes and aromas.

Nosing glass A tulip-shaped glass used to taste whisky. It has a narrow opening so that the whisky can be swirled, allowing the aromas to rise and become concentrated in the nostrils.

Peat Partially carbonised soil that has been compressed over hundreds of years, peat is used for fuel in some malt kilns in Scotland. When burned, it gives off distinctive smoke that contributes significantly to the aroma of some whiskies, especially those from the Scottish islands.

Patent still Also known as the Coffey still, this provides a continuous process of distillation.

Phenolic Intense flavour created in the malted barley from the burning of peat.

Pot ale Sometimes known as burned ale, this is the liquid left in the wash still after the first distillation in the pot still. It is the residue of the wash after the extraction by distillation of the low wines. Like draff (see page 164), it can also be used for animal feed.

Pot still This is a huge copper kettle; the alcoholic spirit is driven off from the fermented liquid as a vapour and then condensed back to liquid.

Proof Measurement of the strength of spirits, expressed in degrees, calculated using a hydrometer. Although still employed in the USA, the proof system has now been superseded in Europe by a measurement of alcohol strength as a percentage of alcohol by volume.

Quaich A traditional two-handled drinking bowl that has, over time, become synonymous with the communal drinking of whisky, especially in Scotland.

(Cath Harries)

Reflux During distillation some of the heavier flavours with comparatively high boiling points condense from vapour back into liquid form before leaving the still and are redistilled – this is known as 'reflux'. The greater the degree of reflux, the lighter and cleaner the spirit produced.

Rummager Apparatus fitted inside a direct-fired copper pot still, consisting of rotating arms carrying copper chain mesh that prevents solid particles in the wash sticking to the bottom; rummagers are not widely used nowadays.

Run The flow of spirit from a still during a specific period of distillation.

Rye Grain used in whisky making, especially in the USA, where rye whiskey was once more popular than bourbon.

Single-cask Whisky that is the product of just one distillation run, from just one individual cask, from just one distillery. It is usually bottled at cask strength, typically 62.5% ABV, rather than the more usual 40% ABV.

Single-malt Whisky that is made of 100% malted barley at a single distillery location but from more than one cask.

Sláinte maith A drinking toast in Gaelic meaning 'good health'. When one person says 'Sláinte maith' (pronounced *slahnje vay*) the response is 'Sláinte mór' (pronounced *slahnje vor*).

Speyside The region of north-east Scotland that is home to approximately half of all Scottish malt whisky distilleries.

Spirit safe The spirit safe was invented by Septimus Fox during the early 1820s, and its use became compulsory in 1823; in the UK spirit safes carry padlocks, placed there by HM Customs and Excise to prevent anyone siphoning off the new make. A spirit safe, a box made of brass and glass within which cutting takes place, encloses the tail or outlet pipe of the worm or condenser. It allows the stillman to watch the flow of spirits or feints, to test for quality and strength, and to route the liquid to the spirit receiver or feints receiver as appropriate – all without having direct physical contact with the spirit.

Steep The vessel in which barley is soaked or steeped during malting.

Still Be it a pot or continuous type, a still works on the principle that alcohol boils at a lower temperature than water and is driven off as vapour, leaving behind the water; the alcohol is then condensed back into liquid form. The name derives from the Latin *stillare* and means 'to drip'.

Stillman The person responsible for managing the still.

Straight A term used in the USA to signify that a whiskey has been aged for at least two years, as in 'Straight Bourbon Whiskey'.

Tennessee Tennessee whiskey is made in the eponymous US state and is characterised by a charcoal filtration process (known as the Lincoln process) that is said to produce a purer, smoother drink.

Top dressing A blending term used to denote high-quality malts that are known to marry well and are used to give a blended whisky depth and character.

(Cath Harries)

Triple distillation The practice of distilling whisky three times rather than the usual twice. It is a traditional characteristic of Irish whiskey, and also of Scottish Lowland whisky making.

Tun A large vessel in which mashing takes place, usually known as a mash tun. However, in a distillery the tun room is home to the washbacks.

Uisge beatha The word 'whisky' derives from *uisge*, which is an abbreviation of *uisge beatha*, the Scots Gaelic for 'water of life'.

Valinch A large pipette used to draw a spirit sample from a cask.

Vatted malt Sometimes referred to as pure malt or blended malt, a vatted malt is where a number of single malts are blended together, but without grain whisky being added.

Wash The alcoholic liquid (typically 7–8% ABV) produced during the fermentation process that is sent to the wash still for the first distillation.

Washback The large tub or vessel in which the fermentation process takes place in a distillery.

Worm A coiled pipe surrounded by cold water in which the distilled spirit vapour is condensed, to be collected via the spirit safe. The vapour cools and reverts to liquid, known as 'low wines' (see page 165). When the evaporation process finishes a residue known as 'pot ale' is left at the bottom of the still; similar to draff, pot ale is also used as animal feed.

Wort A warm, sugary solution that contains the soluble sugars from the malted grist.

Yeast The living micro-organism that is vital for the fermentation process – without it there would be no whisky. Yeast feeds on the sugary wort and produces carbon dioxide and alcohol.

THIS STEEL STRUCTURE IS DESIGNED
TO CARRY
BUTTS WITH BUTTS
STOWED ON TOP
ERECTED BY
REDPATH BROWN & Cᵒ Lᵀᴰ
GLASGOW — 1937.

(Cath Harries)

CHAPTER 3

WHISKY APPRECIATION

Tasting whisky

Whisky – one word, six letters (sometimes seven). But within each glass there is an alphabet of tastes and sensations, history and delectations. Put them together and the letters become words, sentences and a soaring, sonorous thesis.

There is much more to whisky than just a distilled spirit in a glass. Forget the images in old black-and-white movies where angst-ridden characters down a glass in one swift, unappreciative swallow. Whisky, with its history and pride, deserves much more than that.

Good tasting is the key to unlocking the conundrum of what is in a glass. Like fine music or a piece of memorable theatre, each moment needs to be savoured, and then there is the aftermath when only the memories linger, like the fading echo of choral music around a medieval cathedral. As the ancient Greek philosopher Aristotle said: 'The whole is greater than the sum of its parts.'

Writing notes at each stage of the tasting process will add to your appreciation, along with all that you know about the whisky. Over time your notes will chart your journey to the very heart of whisky land.

GLASS CLASS

It all begins with the glass. Go to a whisky tasting and you will normally find that a standard glass is used, specifically to focus your attention on the colours, aromas and alcoholic sensations found within every whisky.

Glasses can come in many shapes and sizes, and each will mould the flavours and sensations of the drink within the glass. But to learn to drink wisely, choose a clear glass snifter, sherry copita or a tulip. These are the auditoriums for whisky theatre. Such glasses have an elegant vase shape that helps the stars of whisky's drama – the colours, aromas and congeners – to reach their audience.

▼ **A good whisky tasting usually involves many different glasses.** (Glenfarclas)

▲ **A gentle swirl of whisky in a glass helps release its character.**

(Glenfarclas)

THE EYES HAVE IT

Some drinkers will always start by reading the label on a bottle of whisky, where there is indeed much important information about the spirit within.

Most of us do not drink in a darkened room from a dark glass. So our first observation of a well-poured whisky will be its colour. Appearance is not everything, but in a sense we do drink with our eyes, our visual sense whetting the appetite and invigorating the taste buds in anticipation. What is the colour of the whisky? Sunset over the Pacific? Golden, flaxen or even well-polished? Much-loved old brown shoes?

Tilt and swirl the glass and let the whisky coat its surface. This permits greater evaporation and thus enhances the aroma. Watch and wait and watch, as the liquid runs back down the side of the glass – this is known as the 'legs' of the whisky. If the legs are thin and run quickly, then the whisky is likely to be younger or lighter. If the legs are slow and thick, then it may be a heavier or older whisky.

NOW THE NOSE HAS IT

Slowly, carefully take a sniff. Do not rush. Savour the moment. The nose can distinguish and discriminate between myriad aromas – more than 1,000 of them – and picks up many tastes that one's tongue cannot detect. It is the nose that leads to a sensation of flavour and memory. In his novel *À la recherche du temps perdu* ('In search of lost time') the French writer Marcel Proust described a character vividly recalling long-forgotten memories from his childhood after smelling a tea-soaked madeleine biscuit.

Now think whisky. Is it peaty or fruity? Does it have hints of

▶ **Before taking a sip let your nose do some work.** (Cath Harries)

sherry? Cinnamon, hay, dried fruit, leather, charcoal, salt, port or wood-burning? For just a moment resist taking a sip and let the whisky aromas swirl and your nose do its work.

TASTE TOUR

Take a small sip. What does it feel like in your mouth? Does it live up to the information you established with your nose? Before you swallow, let the whisky work its way around your mouth, where you have an array of sensitive taste buds that can detect salt, sweet, bitter, sour and umami (a Japanese word meaning 'pleasant savoury taste'). Is it fruity, sweet or dry? What other flavours can you detect? Perhaps there are different fruits or notes of vanilla or other spices? Is it warming? Is the finish short, medium or long?

Above all, take your time. A drink that has taken many years to get from the field to the glass deserves to be appreciated and treated with respect.

WATER WORKS

Now is the time to add a few drops of water – about 10 drops for a 20ml measure of whisky – and take another sip.

▼ A drop of water helps to unlock a whisky's character.

(Cath Harries)

Regardless of your personal preferences about drinking whisky, water is the key to the soul of a whisky. It opens up the drink and helps it to reveal its true self.

The addition of a little water disrupts the alcohol/water balance in the whisky. Alcohol-rich clusters of molecules burst and water-insoluble components escape into the air, creating a change in what the nose perceives. Expect to find more citrus and fruity flavours.

Add more water – one part water to two parts spirit – and the whisky starts to break down, releasing even more of the volatile oils and allowing large water-soluble molecules to manifest themselves as a visible haze. On sipping, the whisky will taste smoother, even creamy, as the large water-insoluble clusters are sensed on the tongue.

WHISKY GALORE

The best way to enjoy a whisky is to be in good company. The joyful sipping of a dram has fuelled many a good conversation. Whisky indeed is a social lubricant. It is much more than an alcoholic liquid in a glass, and one that, with a little more knowledge, can be enjoyed even more.

▼ Always make sure water is available at every tasting.

(Cath Harries)

HOW TO READ A SCOTCH WHISKY LABEL

Reading a whisky label is not difficult and it can add to the fun of enjoying a dram. To make sure that what you are drinking is the real deal, the Scotch Whisky Association has developed a set of rules for labelling to make sure that what it says on the label is actually in the bottle. Our example is a Tamdhu.

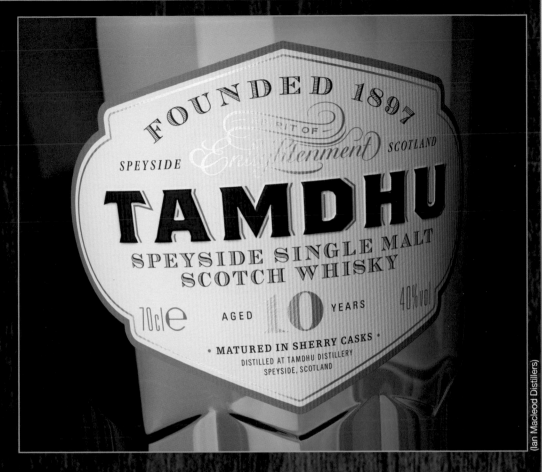

(Ian Macleod Distillers)

1 The distillery's name will be shown, be it from an operating or closed distillery.

2 The location and region of the whisky will usually be stated – in this case Speyside.

3 It is compulsory for every Scotch whisky to indicate on the front label the style of whisky it is: the official terms are Single Malt Scotch Whisky, Single Grain Scotch Whisky, Blended Scotch Whisky, Blended Malt Scotch Whisky or Blended Grain Scotch Whisky.

4 The term 'Single Malt' shows that the whisky has come from one distillery using only malted barley. A blended whisky is made from different single-malt whiskies mixed together.

5 Single malts show the age of the entire contents, whereas a blended whisky will show the age of the youngest constituent. Sometimes distillers show the

bottling date, although this has little point because spirit does not mature in the bottle. Increasingly there are whiskies going on sale without any age statement, but it would be wrong to assume that these are young whiskies.

6 Many distillers state the type of casks used for maturing. Old sherry or bourbon casks are commonly used, but port and wine casks are other possibilities.

7 The alcohol by volume (ABV) should be shown. To be classified as a Scotch whisky it must be at least 40% and it will have been diluted with Scottish water when it was bottled. Cask-strength whiskies will be stronger, typically 65%, but they can range between 45–75%. The ABV gives a reasonable indication of the body of the whisky, the way the whisky feels in your mouth: a whisky of 40–42% will often be described as thin-bodied; 43–48% is medium-bodied; and stronger still is full-bodied.

Whisky cocktails

Whisky is neat on its own – but it is also pretty good as the base spirit in a cocktail. The very best mixologists (cocktail makers) know how to make a drink really shake, rattle and roll by jiggering and muddling different whiskies and flavours.

A good cocktail has that essential drinkability that makes an evening go with a zing. Some whisky cocktails provide a sparkling uplift while others are richer, fuller and require contemplative attention. A good cocktail has balance and is right for the moment.

The slavish following of a recipe that just says 'add 25cl of a branded whisky' will often disappoint. But with so many whiskies to choose from, and knowing the notes in a whisky's scale, you are better informed about what it can add to the chorus of tasters in a cocktail. Is it peaty, does it have vanilla flavours or notes of sherry, leather or even tobacco?

▼ **To make the best cocktails, understand your whiskies.**
(Cath Harries)

SOME FAMOUS WHISKY COCKTAILS

Whisky Sour

Ingredients
- 50ml whisky (bourbon is often used)
- 25ml lemon juice
- 25ml egg white (optional)
- 15ml sugar syrup
- Dash of Angostura bitters

Is this the perfect cocktail? Deceptively simple, it is a refresher in a glass that really allows a whisky to be the star. It is the perfect cocktail for a favourite whisky, and it is great fun to see how it changes with different whiskies.

Like all great cocktails it has the three essential elements: a base spirit, something sweet and something bitter. The key is balance – the harmonious melding of the ingredients into a chorus of harmony – and the fun comes in trying different whiskies and seeing how they change the cocktail.

A drink with a long pedigree, Whisky Sour appeared in America in 1862, when it was included in Jerry Thomas' *Bartenders Guide*.

To make a Whisky Sour, get out the cocktail shaker, put in all the ingredients and shake, then add ice and shake again until your eyes rattle and roll. Now strain the liquid into a chilled glass – some people like to pour it over ice. Put on your favourite music, turn it up loud and enjoy the drink.

Manhattan

Ingredients
- 50ml whisky
- 12.5ml red vermouth
- 12.5ml extra dry vermouth
- 10ml maraschino cherry syrup
- Two dashes of orange bitters
- Dash of Angostura bitters
- Dash of sugar syrup (optional)

Legend has it that this cocktail was conceived in the early 1870s in the Manhattan Club in New York for a banquet hosted by Jennie Jerome, later to be Lady Randolph Churchill, Winston Churchill's mother.

To make a Manhattan, simply add all the ingredients together and stir on ice. Then strain the liquid and pour it into a chilled glass. Garnish with a twist of orange zest and a maraschino cherry.

▲ Theatre is an essential part of a well-made whisky cocktail. (Jameson)

▼ With long histories, whisky sour and Manhattan are two classic whisky cocktails. (Jameson)

Rusty Nail

Ingredients
- 50ml whisky
- 25ml Drambuie

Named after its colour, the Rusty Nail was devised in the late 1930s but it did not acquire its current name and popularity until it became a drink of choice for the famed Rat Pack – the fast-living singers whose members included Frank Sinatra, Dean Martin and Sammy Davis Jr.

The method is to fill a tumbler with ice cubes, then gently pour in the whisky and Drambuie, and stir. Garnish with lemon peel or a cinnamon stick.

Old Fashioned

Ingredients
- 50ml whisky
- Three dashes of orange bitters
- Dash of Angostura bitters
- 15ml sugar syrup

The Old Fashioned originated at the Pendennis Club in Louisville, Kentucky, in the mid-1880s and later made its way to the Waldorf Astoria Hotel in New York. Only later was the practice of 'muddling' adopted in making this cocktail: muddling, which is thought to have been a way of covering the taste of poor alcohol during the Prohibition era, means to combine ingredients (usually in the bottom of a mixing glass) by pressing them with a muddler (usually a wooden pestle shaped like a small baseball bat).

To make this classic cocktail, muddle an orange slice in a tumbler and remove. Add one dash of Angostura bitters and three dashes of orange bitters. Add three ice cubes. Add half of the whisky and stir well. Add two more ice cubes. Add the other half of the whisky and stir well. Add two more ice cubes. Add the sugar syrup (sugar will do) and stir well. Pour, and garnish with a twist of orange zest.

▼ **Attention to detail helps create great cocktails.** (Beam Suntory)

Whisky Royale

Ingredients

- 25ml whisky
- Dash of apple schnapps (or clear apple juice)
- Ginger ale
- Green apple, sliced
- Crushed ice

Half fill a chilled champagne flute with crushed ice. Pour in the whisky and then the apple schnapps. Top up with ginger ale. Place a slice of green apple into the drink.

Highball

Ingredients

- 50ml whisky
- Ginger ale
- Dash of Angostura bitters
- Orange wedge

Glamour in a glass: the name is believed to have been coined in the dining cars of American trains pulled by steam locomotives, on which boiler pressure was indicated by the height of a ball on a pole.

The drink is quick to make. Fill a highball glass with a tower of ice cubes. Add the whisky. Top up with ginger ale. Add a few drops of Angostura bitters. Garnish with an orange wedge.

Hot Toddy

Ingredients

- 50ml whisky
- 5ml runny honey
- Lemon juice
- Boiling water

A cure for many of nature's ills, Hot Toddy is perfect for warming the heart and body on a cold day. Stir the whisky and honey with a squeeze or two of lemon juice in a heat-proof glass, then fill the glass with boiling water and drink while warm.

HOW TO MAKE AN IRISH COFFEE

Like Irish whiskey, Irish coffee has come to epitomise Ireland. It is a drink that mixes sophistication and simplicity together in equal measure. Using Bushmills, Powers, Jameson or Tullamore gives an Irish coffee authenticity, but it is fun to experiment with other whiskies – not necessarily Irish ones – as well.

Ingredients

- 25ml Irish whiskey of your choice.
- 120ml strong, freshly brewed dark roast Arabica coffee
- Two teaspoons of brown sugar
- Fresh half-whipped cream

1 Pre-heat a clear, stemmed glass with very hot water. Empty the water, and add the brown sugar.

2 Add coffee and whiskey to the still-warm glass. Stir well, then wait for the mixture to settle.

3 Take a hot teaspoon and pour the lightly whipped fresh cream slowly over the back of the spoon. Sip and enjoy.

(Tim Hampson)

HOW TO MAKE A BOBBY BURNS

A Bobby Burns is a version of one of the world's great cocktails, the Manhattan, but with a Scottish twist. Originally it may not have been made to commemorate Scotland's favourite poet, Robert Burns, but today the cocktail is often served on 25 January – his date of birth. The cocktail is a favourite of Ernest Reid, the award-winning bar manager of Boisdale Whisky Bar in London's Canary Wharf. Like many classic cocktails, there are many variations on the theme of a Scotch whisky base and vermouth.

Equipment
- Mixing glass (it could be a pint beer glass)
- Bar spoon
- Strainer
- Lots of ice
- Sazerac cocktail glass

Ingredients
- 50ml Speyside single-malt whisky
- Dash of Angostura bitters
- Dash of Peychaud's bitters
- 15ml Bénédictine
- 15ml Rosso Vermouth Antica
- Twist of orange

1 Before you prepare the cocktail in the mixing glass, fill the serving glass – a Sazerac glass is ideal – with ice in order to chill the glass.

2 Add bitters to the mixing glass. Angostura is concentrated bitters, a botanically infused mixture made of water, alcohol, herbs and spices. Peychaud's is made from the root of the gentian plant and is comparable to Angostura but with a lighter body, sweeter taste and more floral aroma.

3 Add whisky, in this case a Glenmorangie Lasanta, which has been aged for ten years in Jack Daniel's Tennessee Whiskey barrels and finished for two years in sherry casks.

4 Add Bénédictine, a French herbal liqueur developed by Alexandre Le Grand in the 19th century.

5 Add Rosso Vermouth Antica. Vermouth, a key ingredient in many classic cocktails, is a fortified wine flavoured with various botanicals, including roots, barks, flowers, seeds, herbs and spices.

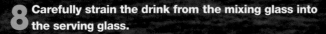

6 Fill the mixing glass with ice and thoroughly stir the ingredients.

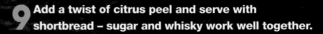

7 Before using the strainer, pour away the ice and excess water from the serving glass, and dry it.

8 Carefully strain the drink from the mixing glass into the serving glass.

9 Add a twist of citrus peel and serve with shortbread – sugar and whisky work well together.

(Cath Harries)

Whisky and food

Wine, beer and cider are often considered to be the perfect partners to fine food, but whisky in all its worldwide manifestations also offers a great range of tastes, aromas and flavours.

I remember the first time I ate a meal with someone who drank whisky with his food. An American publisher in Europe for a conference and exhibition, he ordered a different whisky with each course. He asked the waiter for the list of whiskies and read it with enthusiastic intensity. He carefully choose one and then asked for a small jug of water – 'tap is fine'. He swirled the glass, looking at the legs of the drink before gently, softly breathing in the aromas, almost caressing the drink. Then he took a sip, before adding a dash of water – 'that's just to douse the fire a bit'.

I wish I could remember precisely what he had ordered, but there was a Speyside and then an Islay, and then I do recall that he finished off his meal with a triple-distilled whiskey from County Antrim – Bushmills. He finished his last drink with a smile of supreme satisfaction and announced that he was going to take some bottles of this jewel from the Emerald Isle home with him.

It was some years before I chanced upon a whisky and food dinner again. This time the hosts were staff from the Scotch Whisky Association. The rules of the game were that they could not promote an individual brand, so each whisky that accompanied a course was unknown and in fact not even divulged afterwards – but they were secret ciphers into the world of whisky and food matching.

The first whisky was light and floral, with a clean, fresh taste. It was a perfect partner to a slice of marinated salmon, which was infused with the same delicate fragrance as in the glass. Could it have been a Speyside whisky, possibly a Knockando?

The main course was luscious slices of seared sirloin and a smooth cream sauce. Its partner was an intense smoky, fruity classic, with notes of chilli and peat. Perhaps it was a Talisker from the Isle of Skye?

The meal was finished with a Highland fling, a plate of Scottish artisanal cheeses. Scotland has many fine cheeses made with milk from cow, ewe and goat, and our whisky was full of sherry and fruit flavours with notes of raisins. Could it have been a Blair Athol from Pitlochry in Perthshire?

The basis of a good pairing is balance. A good way to start is to discover for yourself what pairs best with a particular whisky. What are its flavour characteristics? What traits can the palate detect – vanilla, tobacco, soft fruits?

But avoid matching like with like, such as sweet with sweet, and instead seek complementary flavours. A salty blue cheese might work well with a smooth, silky whisky, while a creamy chocolate dessert might suit a spicy whisky that is rich in tannins.

You can take one of your favourite whiskies and think of a dish that might complement it. An easy-going, soft-shoed whisky might go well with the lightness of chicken or even fish, but a robust whisky – one full of flavours of spice, peat and smoke – will need a heartier partner.

The partnership can be made a true marriage if a little of the whisky is used to flavour the accompanying food. A dry

◄ **Macallan Amber, Sienna and Ruby are respectively paired with chowder, duck and a tart with pistachio ice cream.** (Macallan)

whisky could work with freshly opened oysters, while a sweet whisky might cut through the tongue-tingling heat of a hot, spicy curry.

One general rule when devising a whisky menu is to avoid narrowing your choices. For the various courses it is more interesting to select whiskies from different regions or even different countries to provide the most varied flavour profiles.

In Japan, the quest for joyous harmonies is raised to something of an art form. Suntory's Hakushu 12 is light on the nose with flavours of toffee, malt and pine, and it pairs well with the sweetness of toffee biscuits, apple and cream cheese. The Hibiki 12, also from Suntory, is a complex blended whisky that some chefs pair with a traditional Japanese dish called umeboshi, a pickle made from unripe salted plums or apricots. Sour and salty, umeboshi is complemented by the sparkling intricacy of the whisky, with its notes of almonds, sherry and ripe oranges, plus a soft, red, fruity flavour that results from one of the casks used in the blend having been used to store plum wine.

Bourbon, with its high rye content, which gives it a spicy, fruity taste, has the ability to cut through the smoky fattiness of smoked salmon and also goes well with a juicy, grilled steak. Bourbons are flavour heavyweights – often with notes of cherry, caramel, vanilla and smoke – and need equally bold partners, so try rich, spicy barbecue sauces or even strong blue cheeses to complement the heat of the drink.

One of the rising stars of the whisky world is Amrut from India. Its single-malt has a powerful nose of milk chocolate, nuts, spice and light fruit. It harmonises well with rich Cheddar or even a hard, nutty-flavoured French cheese.

Floral, fruity, vanilla, caramel, nutty, sweet, smoky, cereal, aldehyde, woody, resinous, sulphurous, soapy, musty – these are just some of the many notes that play flavour tunes in a whisky.

There is great joy in exploring the boundaries of pleasing food and whisky matches. There are no hard-and-fast rules, but here is a little guidance.

- Light, fragrant whiskies with a touch of sweetness work with sushi, smoked salmon and crab, with soft, creamy cheeses, and with cranachan – a traditional Scottish dessert made with whipped cream and whisky with toasted oatmeal and raspberries.
- Fuller-flavoured whiskies with a touch of peat complement smoky-tasting foods such as mackerel, mussels, venison or bacon.
- Full-bodied, rich whiskies aged in sherry casks suit roasted pork or venison, and fruit cake or gingerbread.
- Strong, peaty whiskies invite bold matches such as scallops and bacon, dark, bitter chocolate, strong blue cheese or very mature Cheddar.

Do not be deterred by those who say whisky and food should never be paired, for they are new-age puritans who are depriving themselves of some of life's greatest joys.

▼ **Good cheese is a perfect partner to a fine whisky.** (Cath Harries)

Whisky recipes

Using wine, beer or even cider in food is certainly not a novelty. But whisky? Yes, a dram of whisky can add complex character to many favourite recipes, so it is well worth taking a bottle from the drinks cabinet and using it in the kitchen.

Depending on the whisky, a dram can bring out the smokiness of smoked food, enhance the flavours of the sea in a fish dish, bring richness to meat dishes and make a sweet dessert even sweeter. In this section I have gathered a few of my favourite whisky recipes.

▲ **The right whisky can pair well with a sweet pudding. The fun is finding out what works.** (Coles Puddings)

Venison fillet steak with whisky sauce

Ingredients
- Four venison steaks
- Marinade:
- 50ml whisky (for marinade)
- 30ml red wine vinegar
- 45ml olive oil
- Zest of lemon peel
- Four shallots or an onion
- Sprigs of parsley, thyme and eight crushed juniper berries
- A good sprinkling of ground black pepper
- 400ml good beef stock
- Knob of butter and 30ml oil for frying
- Large clove of garlic crushed
- 30ml redcurrant jelly
- 15ml whisky (for final spooning sauce)

After mixing together the marinade ingredients, put the steaks in the marinade and leave in a fridge for several hours or even overnight, turning them if necessary.

When you are ready to start cooking, turn the marinade into a pan, add the stock and boil strongly until the liquid is reduced to a volume of about 125ml. Having dried the steaks with kitchen towel, fry them in smoking hot butter and oil for about five minutes each side – longer for well done, shorter for rare.

Remove the steaks from the hot frying pan and leave to rest. Put the garlic into the hot frying pan and soften, then add the strained stock and marinade mix, redcurrant jelly and remaining 15ml whisky, and sizzle until this sauce is well reduced. Adding whisky to the frying pan may well cause it to flame dramatically for a few moments; if this worries you, simply put a lid on the pan and take it off the heat at the first sign of flames.

Spoon the sauce over the steaks. Serve with chips or mashed potatoes and a green vegetable of your choice.

Whisky marinade

Ingredients

- 50ml whisky
- 50ml soy sauce
- Two tablespoons of Dijon mustard
- One large onion, chopped
- 225g brown sugar
- One teaspoon of sea salt
- Dash of Worcestershire sauce
- Ground black pepper to taste

This is a general whisky marinade for use with beef, lamb, chicken or pork, and it also suits shrimps or prawns. To make the marinade, simply stir together all the ingredients. Ideally meat should be marinated overnight in a fridge, but an hour is sufficient for seafood.

Whisky and smoked mackerel paté

Ingredients

- 225g smoked mackerel, skinned and boned
- 50g soft butter
- Juice of one lemon
- Eight drops of Tabasco
- 15ml mayonnaise
- 10ml horseradish sauce
- 30ml whisky

For the whisky, try a smoked Islay. Pound all the ingredients together in a bowl or large mortar, and then press the mixture into a small, straight-sided paté dish or a casserole dish and smooth the top. Cover with greaseproof paper or foil and weigh down with 1kg for at least eight hours in a fridge. After removing the weight and covering, drizzle a little melted butter over the surface. Serve with warm wholemeal toast.

Pancakes with whisky and strawberry sauce

Ingredients

Pancakes (makes 12):

- 110g plain flour
- Pinch of salt
- Two eggs
- 200ml milk
- 75ml water
- 50g butter

Sauce:

- 600ml orange juice
- 15g butter
- Four tablespoons (60ml) of honey
- 90ml whisky
- One punnet of strawberries
- Cream or Greek yoghurt to serve

Pancakes are special at any time of the year, even though

some people choose to eat them only on Shrove Tuesday. However, this recipe is a perfect choice if you want to celebrate the harvesting of the first strawberries of the summer.

To make the sauce, slice the strawberries lengthways into quarters and put them in a saucepan. Pour in the orange juice, add the honey and butter, and bring to the boil. Simmer for five minutes, then add the whisky.

To make the pancakes, sift the flour and salt together, then break the eggs into the middle of the mixture and start whisking. Slowly add in the milk and water mixture, and keep whisking until the batter is smooth – no lumps! If you want smaller, chunky pancakes, add a teaspoon of baking powder to the mix and do not spread the mixture around the frying pan when cooking.

Melt the butter in the frying pan; spoon two tablespoons of the melted butter into the mixture and whisk. Smear the rest evenly round the pan. When the pan is hot, turn down the cooker to a medium heat.

Add two or three tablespoons of the mixture to the pan and quickly tilt it up and down so the mixture spreads. After 30–45 seconds, lift the edges of your pancake to see if it has gone golden brown. If it has, flip it over. The other side will only take about half as long.

If you really want to do things properly, stack your pancakes on a plate between sheets of greaseproof paper and keep them warm by putting the plate over a pan of hot water.

Serve the pancakes topped with the whisky and strawberry sauce and top with cream or Greek yoghurt.

Cranachan

Ingredients

- 275ml thick whipping cream
- 60ml flaked porridge oats or pinhead oatmeal
- 45ml whisky
- 45ml clear honey
- 250g raspberries

This is a much-loved Scottish dessert, especially in the Highlands, that is traditionally served with raspberries.

Heat a large, heavy frying pan and when hot add the oats, stirring constantly. Toast the oats until they have a light, nutty smell and are just beginning to change colour, then remove them from the pan and let them cool.

Whip the cream until it is thick, and fold in the oatmeal, whisky and honey. Spoon into individual glasses or a large glass serving dish and top with raspberries. Chill for an hour in the fridge before serving.

(iStock)

Whisky and chocolate

Anyone looking for a sitting and sipping evening should give whisky and chocolate a go. They are a natural combination as good-quality plain chocolate, with a high percentage of cocoa content, will add to and draw out flavours from a whisky.

The process involves some trial and error, but that is part of the fun. And it should start with the whisky.

Take a small sip of a whisky and let its flavours build in your mouth. Once swallowed, place a small piece of chocolate on your tongue and let it melt. Now experience the twin flavours of whisky and chocolate as they meld together and their heady array of aromas and flavours are released and enhanced.

Before the chocolate has completely disappeared, take a sip of whisky and let it settle on your tongue. This should lead to intense tastes of whisky and chocolate and some interesting and unexpected flavours. Now swallow the whisky and hopefully you will experience some differences in the whisky's flavour profile from the first tasting.

The alcohol in whisky helps to break down the flavours in chocolate, adding to the depth of tastes perceived. The effect is similar to adding a little water to the whisky as it opens up the flavours.

▲ **A little bit of chocolate not only does you good, but it can open up the flavours in a whisky.** (Tim Hampson)

TASTES FOUND IN CHOCOLATE

It helps if you are able to describe chocolate in a similar manner to the sensations you find in whisky. The finest chocolates come with 'terroir'. The very best come from cocoa beans grown in western Africa, the Caribbean, Ecuador, Java, Madagascar and Venezuela.

■ **Bitter-sweet chocolate (70% cocoa or more)** This has the most intense chocolate flavour. Look for bitter, roasted, fruit, earthy, woody and nutty notes. The aftertaste can be bitter.

■ **Milk chocolate (30–45% cocoa)** This is milder and sweeter because it is made with milk and has a higher sugar content than the darker varieties. See if you can discern brown sugar, milk, cream, cocoa, vanilla, honey, caramel, nutty and malt flavours.

■ **White chocolate (0% cocoa)** This, in fact, does not contain chocolate, but includes the milk and vanilla used in milk chocolate. These ingredients give it a variety of sweet notes, including cream, milk, honey, vanilla, caramel and fruit.

Cigars with spirit

Wholly smoke, how about a cigar to go with the whisky? Most people no longer smoke, but for those who do there is something entrancing about the rise and smell of swirling cigar smoke, especially if it is paired with a favourite dram.

(iStock)

A cigar with a whisky makes a great combination. As a general rule the fuller-bodied, stronger cigars, such as a Bolivar, go well with a heavyweight whisky from Islay, such as a Bowmore, Ardbeg or Laphroaig. Alternatively, a lighter Speyside or Lowland whisky might work well with a Romeo y Julieta, the cigar that was favoured by Sir Winston Churchill.

When matching it is usually best if some characteristics in the cigar can also be found in the whisky. The first puff of the cigar will tell you if it is going to be light or heavy in style, or somewhere in between. Now see if you can marry the sensation with the finish and feel of a favourite dram.

As with pairing a whisky with food, there are two approaches. One is to try to achieve complementary flavours, the other is to seek out flavours that create contrast.

Time is of the essence – and lots of it. To fully appreciate a cigar's flavour, puff on it only every minute or so. There is no such thing as a quick cigar. Do not inhale, but focus on the symphony of flavours. In the same way, sip and savour your whisky and concentrate on assessing how its flavour caresses and blends with the taste of the cigar.

Smoking in bars is banned in many parts of the world and smokers therefore have to seek out places where they can still enjoy a puff, but some hotels and whisky bars do offer somewhere where cigars smokers can indulge their passion.

A fine example in the UK is the Boisdale bars in London – in Belgravia and Canary Wharf – where customers are encouraged to puff on large Havana cigars (see pages 54–59). Smokers head to the Cigar Terrace, and fire up alfresco. The terrace is decorated in Boisdale's trademark tartan and furnished with sofas, armchairs, cushions and rugs. In winter months outdoor heaters and an awning keep the weather at bay and guests visiting the terrace are offered warming cashmere blankets while enjoying their cigars.

In the USA cigar smokers can find plenty of opportunities to enjoy their pleasure while travelling the Kentucky Bourbon Trail. Along the route there are various cigar bars and lounges with walk-in humidors that offer plenty of occasions for cigar smokin', barbecue eatin' and bourbon sippin'.

▼◢ **It might not be politically correct but there is a curious harmony between cigars and whisky.**

(Cath Harries and Kentucky Distillers' Association)

Whisky and health

A tot of whisky not only looks good but it will do you good too. Indeed, enjoyed responsibly, all alcohol encourages social interaction and relaxation. The moderate drinking of whisky is part of a healthy lifestyle and can contribute to a longer life than those who abstain or abuse alcohol.

When consumed responsibly, whisky, just like beer and wine, actually has quite a few positive health benefits for its drinkers.

Some of the health benefits of whisky include its ability to aid weight loss, slow down the onset of dementia, increase heart health, prevent and manage diabetes, boost good cholesterol, help resist cancer, eliminate blood clots and strengthen the immune system.

Drinking whisky in moderation dramatically reduces the risk of heart disease. It also significantly reduces the risk of stroke and other major causes of death. Evidence of the overall health benefits of moderate drinking continues to grow and one recent study has found that those who consume a moderate amount of whisky on a regular basis have an almost 50% lower chance of experiencing a stroke or heart attack.

Moderate drinkers also have a 54% lower chance than abstainers of developing dementia. Studies have actually shown that whisky can successfully boost people's cognitive performance and reduce their chances of developing dementia and Alzheimer's disease.

Moderate drinkers are over 30% less likely to develop type 2 diabetes. A moderate amount of whisky can significantly improve the body's ability to regulate insulin and glucose levels, thereby lowering the possibility of developing diabetes.

Whisky is extremely low in saturated fat, cholesterol and sodium. It is also low in carbohydrates: a small shot of it contains only 0.04g of carbohydrates in the form of sugar, which is immediately transformed into energy as soon as it enters our digestive system, and leads to weight gain in people who consume too much sugar or take insufficient exercise. Whisky can play a modest part, therefore, in a healthy diet.

According to several studies, whisky contains ellagic acid in its structure, which is one of the important antioxidant compounds that destroy cancerous cells.

The old wives' tale that a whisky can help fend off a cold may in fact be true as several studies have found that whisky boosts the immune system. The antioxidants and trace levels of vitamins

▲ **Sipping whisky in convivial surroundings is part of a healthy lifestyle.** (Cath Harries)

in whisky stimulate the immune system, thereby helping to fight off coughs and colds. And if mixed with a little lemon, honey or sugar and hot water, whisky can help relieve an itchy throat.

Another virtue is that whisky is an excellent antiseptic. Hundreds of years ago one of the primary uses of distilled spirits was for cleaning wounds.

Do not forget, however, that drinking too much is harmful. The benefits of having a couple of drinks is easily undone if you drink too much.

▼ **A glass of whisky is good for your heart and well being.** (Scotch Whisky Association)

Taste the music and see the light

Drinking whisky is an experience of the senses and there is clear evidence that the music you listen to and the lighting in the room affects the taste of your favourite dram.

'The light music of whisky falling into glasses made an agreeable interlude,' wrote James Joyce in *Dubliners*, his collection of short stories.

Professor Charles Spence, head of the Crossmodal Research Laboratory at Oxford University's Department of Experimental Psychology, says that the different sensory inputs – sounds, lighting, smells and feel – help to bring out different aspects of whisky. He is working with Condiment Junkie, a design company specialising in 'sensory branding', to study the effects of environment on the taste of whisky. According to the researchers, the right sounds, smells and visuals in a room can enhance flavours in whisky.

As well as work in the laboratory, an experiment was carried out by Spence's team with The Singleton whisky in The Singleton Sensorium, a purpose-built bar with three

▼▲ **The colours and sounds in a room can enhance flavours in whisky.** (Diageo)

different rooms, each with different décor, lighting and soundscape.

'The three rooms had very different environments,' explained Spence. 'There was a grassy room with the noises of nature, a fruity room with red fruits and chiming bells, and a woody room with wood panels and sounds of crackling wood.'

Each room affected the senses in different ways. The first room, the green room, was designed to accentuate the grassy nose of The Singleton, and included a real turf floor and sounds of lawnmowers and birdsong. The second room, the red room, aimed to bring out the sweet, dark berry and dried fruit flavours in the whisky, using curved shapes and the sounds of bells ringing. The final room was created to represent the unique finish of the whisky: sounds included double-bass notes, creaking wood and a crackling log fire, while the scent of cedar wood in the air – and a tree growing in the room! – highlighted the lingering taste of age and wood in The Singleton whisky.

'The results confirm that it really is possible to enhance the drinker's experience by creating a rich multi-sensory environment,' said Spence.

So how do different soundscapes pair with different flavours? According to the researchers, a whisky with some sweetness and flavours of red fruit, such as can be found in a 12-year-old cask-strength Springbank, pairs well with higher-pitched sounds from a piano. In contrast, a whisky with dark chocolate notes, like a Talisker Port Ruighe, pairs with lower-pitched brassy sounds. If the whisky contains hints of lemon, like a Cragganmore, it might pair with a piece of mellow violin music, while orange notes pair with a cello. Bass sounds work with cherry flavours while woodwinds tend to suit herbal notes.

WHISKY PLAYLISTS

So what is the ultimate music and whisky experience? What would be your all-time favourite soundtrack to accompany the perfect dram?

The people at The Glenlivet have paired their family of whiskies with music. So if you uncork a bottle of its 12-year-old you should listen to *Pick Up The Pieces* by Average White Band or *Hold On* by Alabama Shakes. If you reach for the 18-year-old turn up the volume and rock to *Hear My Train a Comin'* by Jimi Hendrix; the explosion of sound matches the explosion of aromas and tastes in the glass. And should you be fortunate enough to have a bottle of 25-year-old The Glenlivet then settle down for 40 minutes and listen to John Martyn's *Solid Air* album in its entirety.

Of course there is no right or wrong answer to which whisky is best with which music because music means different things to different people, but it is fun trying to find out which works best. I think, for what it is worth, that if you want your Islay malt to taste earthy and full-bodied try savouring it

▲ **Put the headphones on. Jazz FM has prepared a playlist of music for whisky drinkers.** (Cath Harries)

to a Tom Jones song, or to add a little zing to your Speyside perhaps go for some Madonna?

AN EXPERT'S PLAYLIST

Stephen Teeling of Teeling Whiskey offers his ultimate whisky and music experience.

■ **Teeling Single Grain pairs with U2's** *Desire*.

■ **Pour a glass of Teeling Small Batch and turn up the volume of Thin Lizzy's** *Whiskey in the Jar*.

■ **The Dubliners singing** *Dirty Old Town* **is the perfect partner for a 21-year-old Teeling Single Malt.**

■ **When sipping a 26-year-old Teeling Single Malt put on Luke Kelly's** *The Auld Triangle*.

■ **And if you are planning a wild evening with a glass of Teeling Poitín, the ultimate music choice has to be the Pogues' version of** *Wild Rover*.

▶ Teeling Whiskey is produced in the first new distillery to be opened in Dublin for over 125 years. (Cath Harries)

Whisky trails

So you have a spirit of adventure and want to search for the perfect whisky? There is much more to whisky than the contents of a bottle – from history and culture to science and technology – and nowadays museums, distilleries, tastings and trails all offer new insights into the world of whisky.

From the source of the water, to the type of cereal used, to the shape of the still, to the wood used for maturation – a tour of a distillery reveals what makes each whisky so different.

Visiting a distillery allows people to indulge their passion for whisky and meet some of the people who contribute to the drink's varied character. Many distilleries welcome visits from whisky fans and have vibrant visitor centres. Some tours have to be booked in advance while others do not require prior notice.

Scotland offers the most scope for the whisky traveller with its concentration of over 100 distilleries and more than 40 of these have facilities for visitors. Many are set in stunning areas of natural beauty and no two distilleries are the same, each having its own distinctive way of doing things and its own story.

A Scotland Whisky initiative (www.scotlandwhisky.com) has created a network of whisky 'embassies' – bars, restaurants and hotels – with fantastic whisky knowledge.

SPEYSIDE WHISKY TRAIL

Scotland's Malt Whisky Trail (www.maltwhiskytrail.com) takes travellers through one of the country's best-known whisky regions, Speyside, which has Scotland's largest concentration of distilleries, many of which are open to the public. The tour follows a route of 70 miles and you do not have to travel far before you see the distinctive pointed chimney tops of a distillery. The route allows the traveller not only to learn more about whisky but also to see one of the most beautiful parts of Scotland.

■ **The Glenlivet** Many travellers take three days to complete the route and begin by visiting The Glenlivet distillery in Banffshire. Admission is free and the guided tour provides an insight into the history of single-malt.

▼ **Scotland has many fine whisky trails and distillery tours.**
(Pernod Ricard)

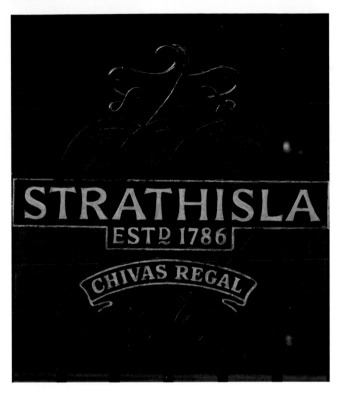

◀▲ **Strathisla is the oldest operating distillery in the Highlands, and one of the most picturesque.** (Pernod Ricard)

■ **Cardhu** It is a short drive north to Knockandu, home to the Cardhu distillery. Take one of the two tours offered to find out more about the only malt whisky distillery pioneered by a woman.

■ **Speyside Cooperage** Continue nine miles towards Dufftown, to the spectacular Speyside Cooperage where barrels are still made from American oak by hand, using traditional methods. Each year around 100,000 casks – barrels, hogsheads, butts and puncheons – are made or repaired here.

■ **Glenfiddich** The Glenfiddich distillery in Dufftown is next, built by William Grant and his family over a period of 18 months, the first drops of whisky having flowed from the stills on Christmas Day in 1887. Tours of the Balvenie distillery can also be arranged and commence at Glenfiddich.

■ **Glen Grant** The Glen Grant distillery is in nearby Rothes. This is the only Scotch whisky distillery that is named after its founding owners and it has a delightful Victorian woodland garden.

■ **Strathisla** It is a 20-minute drive from Rothes to Keith, where a tour of the Strathisla distillery can be taken. This is the oldest operating distillery in the Highlands and dates back to 1786. Here more can be learned about the art of blending as the distillery produces a range of Chivas Regal blended whiskies.

■ **Glen Moray** Next comes Glen Moray distillery in Elgin.

From here, many people drive 20 minutes to Forres and the Benromach distillery, which is home to the world's first fully certified organic single-malt.

■ **Dallas Dhu** After a final ten-minute drive people can complete the exploration of the Malt Whisky Trail at Dallas Dhu Historic Distillery, which produced whisky from 1899 to 1983, when a water shortage following a prolonged drought led to its closure.

SCOTCH WHISKY EXPERIENCE

No visit to Edinburgh would be complete without a trip to the Scotch Whisky Experience (www.scotch-whisky-experience.co.uk). This spirited insight into the world of Scotland's most famous export takes you from its cottage industry beginnings to the global success it is today.

Here you can take a swirling, bubbling barrel ride through a replica distillery as you become part of the whisky-making process. Along the way you will hear the stories behind the craft of whisky making. The tours finish with a close-up look at the world's largest collection of Scotch whisky and the chance to taste a malt or two.

A LITTLE BIT OF THE IRISH

Ireland, where they make their whiskey with an 'e', is credited with having invented whisky so it should be a number one destination for any fan. When the great whisky traveller Alfred

▲ Many whiskey travellers to Ireland visit Cork to see the
Jameson Experience. (Jameson)

▲ **The Old Jameson Distillery in Dublin has a grand bar area.**
(Tim Hampson)

Barnard visited Ireland in 1886 he found 28 distilleries, but only
two of these are still in full operation today.

■ **The Jameson Experience** The Jameson Experience is
located in Midleton, County Cork in the old Cork Distilleries
Company premises. It operated for 150 years, from 1825
until 1975, when the workers clocked off on a Friday in
July, to start work in the new Midleton distillery the following
Monday. Thankfully, the old distillery was kept intact and
has been preserved as a tourist attraction.

■ **Irish Whiskey Museum** A busy corner of bustling Grafton
Street, opposite the main entrance to Trinity College, is
home to the Irish Whiskey Museum in the centre of Dublin.
Although distilling has never taken place on the site, this is a
first-class visitor attraction that tells the story of the rise, fall

and 21st-century renaissance of the Irish whiskey industry. A
visit ends with a tasting of some modern-day classics.

■ **Old Jameson Distillery** Located on the original site of
John Jameson's distillery in Bow Street, Dublin, this was
Ireland's most famous distillery for nearly 200 years, until
its closure in 1971, when distilling was transferred to the
Midleton distillery. For many years the site lay abandoned,
but today, once again, it is a hub of activity, welcoming
visitors from all over the world.

■ **Kilbeggan** The Kilbeggan Distillery Experience is situated
in the centre of Ireland in the small town of Kilbeggan in
County Westmeath. Established in 1757 and the oldest
continually licensed distillery in Ireland, the Kilbeggan
distillery closed in 1954 but is now once again distilling and
maturing whiskey, and is open to visitors all year round.

■ **Tullamore D.E.W.** Located in Tullamore, County Offaly,
the museum and visitor centre is based in a restored
19th-century warehouse that was the original home of

▼ The Old Jameson Distillery, Dublin is one of the city's most
popular visitor attractions. (Tim Hampson)

Tullamore D.E.W. Irish whiskey. It opened in 1829 and was to become, until its closure in 1954, one of Ireland's most successful and famous distilleries. The initials D.E.W. are those of Daniel E. Williams, who worked his way up from the bottom, shovelling malted barley, to become the distillery's owner in the late 19th century.

■ **Bushmills** This is Ireland's oldest working distillery in County Antrim, Northern Ireland. Situated close to the Giant's Causeway, it has a popular visitor centre.

KENTUCKY BOURBON TRAIL

Take the famed Kentucky Bourbon Trail (http://kybourbontrail.com) through the heart of bourbon country and you can visit eight of the state's bourbon distilleries – including Maker's Mark, Jim Beam and Woodford Reserve – on a journey that will take three leisurely days. The trail is not a geographic route, so there is no official beginning or end to it; people just go where the spirit takes them.

Kentucky is home to 95% of America's distillation, ageing and bottling of bourbon, a corn-based, caramel-coloured sipping spirit. It is big business for the state. But more than industry, bourbon is a culture, a history and heritage built by generations since the late 18th century.

■ **Evan Williams** Located on Louisville's historic Whiskey Row, this distillery celebrates the legacy of Evan Williams, Kentucky's first distiller.

■ **Four Roses** Built in 1910, Four Roses distillery features unique Spanish mission-style architecture rarely seen in Kentucky, and is listed on America's National Register of Historic Places.

■ **Heaven Hill** This is America's largest independent family-owned producer of bourbon and was founded after the end of Prohibition by the Shapira family.

■ **Jim Beam** This is the largest producer of bourbon, bottling a staggering 90 million bottles of spirits annually.

■ **Maker's Mark** Production of Maker's Mark started in 1954, after its originator, T. William 'Bill' Samuels Sr, purchased the distillery known as Burks.

■ **Town Branch** Founded in 2000, this is part of the Alltech Lexington Brewing and Distilling Company.

■ **Wild Turkey** In 1869 the Ripy brothers built a distillery in Tyrone, Kentucky, consolidated the current facility by 1905, and resumed distilling after Prohibition.

■ **Woodford Reserve** The oldest and smallest distillery in Kentucky traces its origins to 1797, when Elijah Pepper began distilling in Woodford County.

KENTUCKY BOURBON TRAIL CRAFT TOUR

Those with a spirit of adventure can also tackle the Kentucky Bourbon Trail Craft Tour and visit some of the new wave of smaller distillers in the 'Bluegrass State'.

▲ **A tour of the Kentucky Bourbon Trail takes in some of the most famous whiskey names in the world.** (iStock)

■ **Barrel House** Located on the site of the old James E. Pepper Distillery in historic Lexington, Barrel House Distilling makes, in addition to its bourbon, Devil John Moonshine in honour of a legendary Civil War soldier, lawman and moonshiner.

■ **Corsair Artisan** Founded in 2010, Corsair Distillery is a leader of the growing craft spirits movement, especially for whiskey. Its eclectic output ranges from an oak-smoked wheat whiskey to Triticale whiskey, which uses a new grain variety created by crossing species of wheat and rye.

■ **Limestone Branch** Brothers Steve and Paul Beam founded the distillery in Lebanon and have attempted to create the distillery as it would have been when operated by their forebears, who distilled in the state in the 18th century.

■ **MB Roland** This distillery was founded by Paul and Merry Beth ('MB') Tomaszewski in 2009 as the state's first complete grain-to-glass craft distillery.

■ **New Riff** New Riff Distilling in Newport opened in 2014 and its focus is on making bourbon and rye whiskey. Its production is small, making only a small number of barrels each day.

■ **Old Pogue** The original Pogue distillery was established in 1876 and today the bourbon-making tradition is carried forward by Pogues of the fifth and sixth generations.

■ **Silver Trail** Owner and head distiller R. Spencer Balentine makes old-fashioned moonshine, based on a family recipe, and calls it LBL ('Land Between the Lakes') after the nearby designated National Recreation Area.

■ **Wilderness Trace** Opened in 2013, this distillery's initial line includes a bourbon, a rye, a vodka and a sorghum-based spirit.

■ **Willett** The construction of this distillery began in 1935 and at some time during the 1970s it started to make ethanol for fuel rather than whiskey. Happily it is back making drinking spirit again.

JOHNS
John Distilleries
has been declared the
4th largest liquor company
in India.
"Original Choice" brand of
Indian whisky is 2nd fastest
growing regional brand of
whisky in the world and
14th largest liquor brand
in the world.
"Big Banyan" premium wines
are world acclaimed in
11 distinct varietals of white,
red, rose and dessert wines,
as wine making mastery of
Lucio Matricardi, Italy.

Whisky shows and festivals

Master classes, tasting and talks are all part of the fun of whisky shows and festivals around the world. This section provides a few tasters by outlining a few of the myriad events, with the emphasis on whisky's homeland north of the border.

A good example of the range of events for whisky lovers taking place around the world these days is Whisky Live (www.whiskylive.com), a collective of shows at venues around the world. In this book's year of publication, for example, Whisky Live events took place in Australia (Adelaide, Brisbane, Canberra, Melbourne, Perth and Sydney), Belgium (Spa), Indonesia (Jakarta), Israel (Tel Aviv), The Netherlands (The Hague), the UK (London) and the USA (New York and Washington DC).

ENGLAND

Here are two London-based suggestions to nurture and develop your interest in the world of whisky.

- **Whisky Show** This is the UK's biggest whisky event (www.whisky-show.com) and takes place in London during October. It includes tutored tastings and provides an insight into the world of whisky and your chance to ask all those unanswered questions. Many of the master classes are dedicated to one brand or expression.
- **Whisky Squad** The Whisky Squad (www.whiskysquad.com) are Jason Standing, Billy Abbott and Joel Eastman, who come up with themes for informal tastings, sell the tickets and pool the money to purchase the whiskies, sometimes with the support of a brand that will donate an appealing bottle or two. The Squad have come up with lots of fun ways to sip a dram, from whisky tastings in the total

◀ **Whisky shows offer the opportunity to try many rare and unusual drams.** (Cath Harries)

▶ **A good whisky show allows attendees the opportunity to explore the diverse world of whisky.** (Cath Harries)

darkness (Jason had to wear night-vision goggles to pour the whiskies) to a Lowlands tasting one summer evening in London's Green Park.

SCOTLAND

Across Scotland can be found many festivals and events dedicated to the country's national drink. This is the ideal way to discover your favourite malt. People can sample local flavours, take part in a master class and often visit a distillery or two.

■ **Spirit of Speyside** Held annually at the beginning of May, the Spirit of Speyside Festival (www.spiritofspeyside. com) invites visitors to enjoy a wide-ranging programme of whisky-inspired events – some educational, all of them fun. Since its inception in 1999, whisky lovers from all over the world have flocked to it. Visitors are spoiled for choice with a vast range of activities to participate in, from distillery tours and Highland hikes to master-class tastings and blending sessions.

■ **Fèis Ìle** Another May-time festival, Fèis Ìle, otherwise known as Islay Festival of Malt and Music (www.islayfestival. com), was founded in 1986 to celebrate the heritage and culture of Islay, the Hebridean island that boasts 11 whisky

distilleries. This week-long event is a great way to discover the peaty, amber delights from the distilleries of Islay as well as neighbouring Jura. Each distillery holds its own open day, and the week is full of traditional music, ceilidhs, children's shows, guided walks and outdoor activities.

■ **Spirit of Stirling Whisky Festival** Set in Stirling's historic Albert Hall, this one-day event (www. spiritofstirlingwhiskyfestival.co.uk) in May has been enthusiastically received by whisky fans, with over 250 whiskies available for tasting including big names such as The Macallan, Highland Park, Bowmore and Ardbeg.

▼ **Unusual and rare whiskies frequently star at the best whisky shows.** (Cath Harries)

Enjoying whiskey in Ireland

Irish whiskey is in growth. While the country will never return to the heyday of the 19th century, when more than 2,000 stills were regularly fired up, distilleries are opening across the Emerald Isle.

▲ **The Crown is wonderfully atmospheric, with period gas lighting and cosy snugs.** (iStock)

Although all four of the main Irish producers – Jameson, Bushmills, Tullamore and Cooley – are in the hands of large multi-nationals, a grass-roots revival is taking place in the Emerald Isle.

American distiller Alltech, for example, has teamed up with craft brewers Carlow Brewing to begin distilling. Alltech's founder, Pearce Lyons, has Irish roots and sees this venture as an important element in ensuring that Ireland has independent distillers. A visitor centre is planned and is certain to become a significant tourist attraction.

At Tullamore in County Offlay, William Grant is investing in a distillery that will secure the future of the Tullamore D.E.W. brand, returning whiskey making to a village that has been dry for 60 years. On the West Coast the renaissance of Irish whiskey is being led by Dingle Distillery, which is owned by the Porterhouse Group, famed for its pubs in Dublin and elsewhere in Ireland.

BELFAST

The great distillery chronicler Alfred Barnard described Belfast as the Athens of Ireland. He said the city was the most celebrated in Ireland and renowned for the public spirit of its inhabitants. Perhaps that is why it is such a great place to drink whiskey.

Many of the city-centre bars are old, but far from old-fashioned, as they are usually full of people of all ages enjoying conversation, music nights and, of course, good drinks. They are untroubled by canned music – they almost seem untouched by time since the age of Queen Victoria – and people make the intoxicating atmosphere.

The Crown Liquor Saloon

Is this the most famous pub in Northern Ireland? Owned by the National Trust, it recently acquired a certain notoriety when the operator forgot to renew its liquor licence.

The interior, created by Italian craftsmen in Belfast's Victorian glory days, is elaborate and ornate. It is a joy to settle into one if its ten original, carved snugs – irreplaceable Victorian marvels embellished with lions' and griffins' heads – and sample a glass of the hard stuff. Or, if that is not enough, to stand at the long Balmoral Red granite-topped altar bar and enjoy a 'High Class Whiskey'.

The Duke of York

On my visit, as I walked through the door, a man smoking outside told me that Sinn Féin leader Gerry Adams worked here as a barman in the late 1960s. Situated along a narrow, cobbled alleyway in the historic Half Bap area, this pub can be a mad swirl of music, with people singing, clapping and shouting. The energy reverberates around a delightful clutter of Victorian patina and distillery memorabilia.

And then there is the whiskey – more than 500 types. Whiskey is owner Willie Jack's passion. The pub is a rousing tribute to a drop of the Irish with the extensive menu of whiskeys displayed along the ornate shelves, surrounded by décor of antique mirrors and newspaper artefacts.

The Harp Bar

Just a few steps away from the Duke of York, the Harp Bar is another jewel owned by Willie Jack where he can indulge his love of live music and whiskey. Inside it is smart, mixing nostalgia and a love of the past with contemporary chic. Everyone is keen to tell you that Van Morrison sang here on New Year's Eve in 2013 – and he promises to return.

The pub's heady atmosphere is as intoxicating as the contents of the hundreds of whiskey bottles that stand in tribute to the distiller's art. This is Belfast spirit at its best, with the walls and cabinets featuring rare Belfast whiskey. The building's origins as a bonded warehouse – the headquarters of The Old Bushmills Distillery Company – are reflected in various branded mirrors and memorabilia.

The Merchant Hotel

This hotel's bar is gloriously grand: antique Baccarat chandeliers hang from the ceiling and on cold nights a magnificent open fire adds heat to the atmosphere. Regarded by some as the world's best hotel bar, it is a perfect place to enjoy a whiskey cocktail or even a dram softened with a few drops of water. The knowledgeable staff happily talk whiskey and will suggest one to suit your mood.

DUBLIN

There is nowhere better to experience the revival of Irish whiskey than in Dublin. At one time Dublin was one of the giants of the whisky world, and now, with the Teeling Whisky Company, distilling is returning to the city where John Teeling began distilling around 1782. Founded by former Cooley executive Jack Teeling, the new Teeling Whiskey Company has big plans.

Teeling's first whiskey, which was appropriately called Hybrid, was a marriage of two single-malts from Cooley in Ireland and Bruichladdich on Islay, with the two stored together for eight years in oak barrels. Now the company is planning to release a range of blends aimed at discerning drinkers looking for whisky matured for 20 years and more.

The Temple Bar

Temple Bar is one of the great places in Dublin for a traveller looking for the spirit of adventure. Located on the often crowded street of the same name, this looks just to be a small corner bar, but inside it explodes into an expanse of drinking spaces, offering a heady atmosphere of music, oyster dishes, *craic* and whiskey.

The bar's whiskey collection is a long-established selection of rare and interesting whiskeys gathered for decades from all over the world. It all started when the bar used to bottle and label each individual whiskey from the barrel into its own unique bottles. Today this practice is handled by the distilleries, leaving the bar's staff to concentrate on providing customers with Ireland's largest whiskey collection.

The Temple's building was probably built at the start of the 17th century on land recently reclaimed from the sea, a barr on the banks of the tidal River Liffey, by Sir William Temple, who was made provost of Trinity College, Dublin. The Temple family's block of land became known as Temple's Barr or simply Temple Bar.

▼ **Every tourist to Dublin seems to visit the Temple Bar.**
(Tim Hampson)

Whisky magic

Can you pour whisky and make it sit on top of a glass of water? Allan Crumb, tour guide at the Penderyn Distillery in South Wales, can. And as he hates to waste good whisky, he knows how to decant out the water and leave the whisky behind.

Here is a magic trick involving whisky. You will be able to amaze your friends, and perhaps win the odd bet or two, by being able to pour whisky on to water without it mixing. Here is how to do it.

1 Three-quarters fill a whisky glass with water.

(All photos Cath Harries)

2 Place a handkerchief or similar on top of the glass and carefully pour whisky on to it.

3 A good measure of whisky should then sit within the 'cupped' part of the handkerchief.

4 When you carefully remove the handkerchief the whisky should be left floating proudly on top of the water.

5 The trick works because whisky, which is normally 40% ABV, is less dense than water. The whisky is lighter and therefore stays on top of the water. If you are told the trick is a waste of good whisky, carefully put a straw through the layer of whisky and suck out the water below it – and you are left with a whisky in your glass.

CHAPTER 4
MAKING WHISKY

(Cath Harries)